MW00397023

Grieg Lodge Remembers:

Looking Back to World War II

Astri Grieg Fry

Astri Grieg Fry

DEDICATION

To my husband Jim,
for his love and unfailing support

We the children called out when the planes came:
    "Where is mamma?"
And she cried when the bombs fell:
    "Where in God's name are the kids?"

War is not for children and mothers—
    War is for tough men.
No, no, war is not for people,
    War is fear.

War is not for anyone.

    —Norway's Resistance Museum at Akershus, Oslo

AUTHOR'S NOTE

"Why are you doing this?" After starting this book venture, *Grieg Lodge Remembers*, this question arose multiple times. The answer quite simply became: Inquisitiveness.

Several years ago, I noticed that some Grieg Lodge members still reminisced about World War II in Norway when they had witnessed the war as children or young adults, or they had family stories. I began speculating if there was enough material for a book and presented the idea to the Lodge in early 2015.

I was born after the war, but, while growing up in Canada and Norway, I heard firsthand references to the Nazi occupation of Norway from my parents. However, as related in "Kari's Story," they got off fairly lightly. Later, while attending high school at Oslo Handelsgymnasium, my understanding of Noway's role during World War II expanded in Norwegian History and Literature classes. Moreover, there had been a tremendous post-war literary outpouring in Norway. After all, practically everyone had been affected and personal experiences abounded, but with much of this material remaining only in Norwegian. For a while during this year, it seemed constantly that someone would exclaim: "HAVE you read . . . ?" and present me with a stack of books from their private collection. Almost all of these volumes were *på norsk*. Compiling our stories into a book this year, we now offer renewed portrayals of the war in Norway—in English.

Throughout this process, some people have preferred to write their own stories, while others offered records from before. Other stories were collaborations: the contributor talked, I wrote; we revised jointly. While these stories, with some exceptions, are mostly personal recollections, I have strived to check historical facts as this collection has progressed.

The responses and material from Lodge members, family and friends have greatly exceeded my expectations: ranging in scope from scenarios of comic relief all the way to the chilling horrors of the Holocaust. I have felt honored that so many people have entrusted me with their accounts. My original intention was to feature Grieg Lodge members only, focusing on the Norwegian point of view. However, some Lodge members had war experiences in other countries, whereas I have included some extended contacts of my own. These latter stories developed into the last chapter, "Norway and Beyond," featuring some of Norway's Allies during the war: Great Britain, the US, Russia and, during the second half of the war, Italy.

Now, seventy years after the conclusion of World War II, many stories have disappeared or about to do so. Nevertheless, I discovered that many stories lie still just beneath the surface. I'm glad I was inquisitive! *Tusen takk* again to all the contributors, and may our readers find our combined efforts to be enriching!

Astri Grieg Fry
Portland, Oregon
September 2015

CONTENTS

Chapter 1: Eastern Norway

WORLD WAR II IN OSLO, NORWAY
by Aase Barnes and Astri Grieg Fry

I, Aase, was born on 2 February, 1940, the only child of my Isaksen parents. When the war broke out just two months later, there were rumors that Oslo was going to be bombed, and so we stayed with some friends in the country for a few months. Then we returned to our Oslo apartment. We lived on the fourth floor of our building and when the air strike sirens went off, we fled to the basement, bringing with us food, water, flashlights and a first aid kit. Once I was old enough to observe this, it was scary for me to see my parents looking afraid. Altogether we might have been twelve to fourteen people taking refuge down there. Normally this basement was only used for storage. Bicycles were kept there and each family had its own storage booth. During the raids, each person had a chair, but we sat crowded in the narrow passage between the storage booths. It was dark and even though we were underground, there was no feeling of safety. A bomb going off made a sound like a big bang which I can remember hearing from the age of three or four. Bombing was sporadic; sometimes several times during the day or even at night. At other times, there may have been no raids for weeks on end. All the same, the bombing went on throughout the five-year duration of the war.

1

Owning a radio was illegal, but my father listened to his set anyway, which made my mom very nervous. He heard news about the war from neutral Sweden.

Later in the war, in 1943 or 1944, I rode on a bus with my mom to visit some friends who lived on a farm, and to buy eggs and milk from them. On the way back my mom said, "Don't say anything about what we have in our bags, because German soldiers might get on the bus, find out what we have and take it." Nothing happened, but it was scary all the same. We were hungry.

Food being so hard to come by, we might see these signs posted at the grocery stores: "No Milk Today." "No Potatoes." I don't know how my mom prepared food without having any sugar, cream or butter. We ate a lot of potatoes; that is, when we could get them. We did, however, have apples and a community garden where we might have grown carrots and turnips. It was only after the war that I saw, and could eat, a banana for the first time.

My mom was resourceful and made the most of whatever was at hand; for example, for my fourth birthday she sewed me a dress out of what probably was flour sacking. I thought it was beautiful.

In our neighborhood I had some Jewish friends, especially one little Jewish girl my age. One day we saw a truck drive up, stop in front of her apartment and German soldiers from the truck entered her home. They came out with her entire family. My little friend was called over, and they all got on the truck and drove off. Later I was told that

2

they had been taken to a concentration camp from which they never returned as far as I know.

After the war had ended, my parents and my five-year-old self went to Oslo's downtown, along with thousands of others to welcome our returning Norwegian royal family. Our king and crown prince had spent the war exiled in England while other royal family members had resided in the US. Now we could again display and wave our Norwegian flags. We could cheer out loud and sing our national anthem "Ja, vi elsker" once more. I saw that people around us had tears in their eyes. This event took place in June that year, but it felt like a Syttende Mai parade and celebration with the royal family in cortege down Oslo's main street, Karl Johan, flanked by the jubilant crowds.

Even as young as I was during this war, to this day I dislike violent movies so much that I will walk away during graphic wartime movie scenes. On the other hand, I treasure the many good things I have in life. I don't take them for granted, such as my family ties, my friends, a good standard of living, good health, and, since retiring from work, travel opportunities and volunteering in my community.

MY NORDSTRAND SCHOOL YEARS
DURING WORLD WAR II

by Liv A. Hughes and Astri Grieg Fry

9 *April, 1940*. A day of infamy in our history when the Germans began occupying Norway. I, Liv Andersen, was a first grade student and my mother was a teacher. The principal lived on the first floor in a house adjacent to the school with his three university student sons who were like older brothers to me. My mother and I lived upstairs.

10 April, 1940. Rumors were flying that Oslo might be bombed by the Allies. We lived just a few miles to the southeast, in Nordstrand along the Oslofjord. My mother called my grandfather to decide whether or not we should head for our cabin in the Lillehammer area more than 125 miles away. We did not attempt this then which was just as well, due to the presence of German forces there that we knew nothing of in Oslo.

12 April, 1940. On that day German soldiers took over our Nordstrand School. My mother was a single parent. When my nanny and I first witnessed the tramping feet of three hundred marching German soldiers, she became so alarmed that she wanted to flee on the spot. However, in that instance at least, the invaders spent only one night at our school.

Within a year and a half into the war, our school had been requisitioned as a field hospital for the German troops. Therefore our grade school setting was improvisational for the remaining war years. This proved to be a master stroke

4

on the part of our principal, shielding us from the Nazi doctrine that the Germans were determined to impose. Through community efforts, classes were organized and rotated in private homes where we gathered around the dining room table. Depending on where one lived, this could entail a long walk to and fro. Under these circumstances, our curriculum was pared down to reading, writing and arithmetic. We children happily went along with this reduced schedule. Little did we dream how disadvantaged we would be years later when attending middle school and high school. By then we were practically devoid of a foundation in Norwegian history and literature, art, geography, music, religion, PE, shop and home economics. We had considerable catching up to do!

During the war, the following ritual was observed on school days: Norwegian children must not forego their daily cod liver oil supplement, war or no war! And so we lined up, each with her own personal silver christening spoon brought each time from home, as our teacher dispensed the allotted mouthful of *tran*. For our lunch, two students would take turns trudging to a soup kitchen in the vicinity, prepared at the Home for the Deaf, carrying pails for that purpose. We desperately needed whatever nourishment these everlasting soups provided, but to this day I dislike even the memory of barley, vegetable or pea soup. To me, they were watery soups with any trace of broth conspicuously absent. In general, food in the towns was hard to come by during the five-year German occupation. We raised rabbits for food and some people owned pigs. Anyone with access to any plot of earth would grow potatoes, carrots, cabbage, turnips—whatever could be coaxed to grow in our nordic climate.

Whenever we had the opportunity, we took the train to Lillehammer in summer, as passengers in box cars. We stayed for much as four weeks at my grandfather's cabin in Gausdal. Once there, we drove by truck to the remoter dairy farms sitting perched on top of large milk cans. In advance my mother would have visited Vinmonopolet, the government-controlled liquor store in Norway, and stocked up on whatever she could obtain. These commodities were the equivalent of liquid gold for bartering: a bottle of whiskey for this farmer, a bottle of wine for that one; goat cheese, flour, eggs for us. I remember these summer respites as a wonderful time. Good food for a change, maybe even a little beef or pork, and going fishing for mountain trout.

When the sirens went off during the war, we took shelter in the nearest basement. The principal's sons quickly got tired of dashing to the shelter on demand, so they fixed up sleeping accommodations, using the bathtub and whatever benches were available and regularly slept there at night. These air raids continued intermittently throughout the war.

These young university students, however, were rounded up as forced labor. Two of the three were in fact sent to one of the infamous camps, Auschwitz. Somewhere in 1942-43 I wrote them a letter, but received no reply. The grownups around me said only that, given the war situation,

6

it would take a long time for any mail to get through in either direction. Nevertheless, they did survive their concentration camp ordeal. One of them was even able to state ultimately, "You do forgive, but not forget." Following largely in his father's footsteps, by then he was the head of Kristelig Gymnasium, a parochial high school in Oslo.

Similarly to the black market, the German occupation's repression directly gave rise to the Norwegian Resistance Movement. Some was overt, like the wearing of *nisseluer*, the red Norwegian winter caps. This defiance was publicly banned by the Germans by the autumn of 1941; however, a more pressing matter for them was the confiscation of radios. In our immediate area, the teachers were able to hide their radios in a closet in the principal's attic. The closet was duly locked and sealed by the police. This provided some measure of comic relief as the closet could be accessed from above. Norwegians could listen to the news after all, providing vital material for the illegal newspapers. Even my small self played an integral role here. My mother, an enterprising member of the teacher's union and collaborating with the Underground, forwarded these updates from the outside world to other teachers. Her epistles were concealed beneath the jumbled contents of my school backpack with me as liaison. The Nazis never suspected then what I actually carried on my person—and no more did I!

Near our home there were two houses where the local Jews were congregated. One day they had all vanished and the Germans had taken over these buildings.

By this time I was attending fourth grade. Like so many other youngsters, I was underweight, disturbed by people inexplicably disappearing and unnerved due to the air raids. Some children at this time got a hiatus in rural areas. I was one of these lucky ones, possibly through my mother's influence as a teacher. I was sent down-fjord, near Halden towards the Swedish border for the month of April 1944. There I had good food to eat and learned to milk cows. This was such a good experience that I got to return at a later time, glad to help out again with farm chores.

In the fall of 1944, the Germans suddenly showed up at our house, announcing with characteristic curtness, "Tomorrow you'll be out of here. Take what you need and get ready to leave!" We had just received a delivery of firewood; this we removed. Neighbors came to help and remove everything else possible from our home. This included the contraband radios in the attic, now exported thence beneath large maps under the very noses of a myriad of German soldiers in the schoolyard. I kept asking "What is going on?" but got little in the way of adult response. Our belongings were stored in various locations. We moved into a small apartment recently vacated by a teacher, and lived there for the rest of the war.

8 May, 1945. This was the date of the German surrender in Norway. I saw German soldiers riding by on motorcycles with white flags on them. Somehow I no longer felt afraid of them, although I have retained a lasting, if exaggerated, respect for authority figures. On that day our gymnastics team was putting on an end-of-term program for the school. Reverting to what used to be the norm for us, we marched in carrying the Norwegian flags now brought forth from their hiding places—our flags which were banned by the Germans during the war at the risk of deportation or worse. As we marched in, everyone spontaneously started singing our national anthem "Ja, vi elsker," and there wasn't a dry eye in the house. This represented the crowning moment not only then, but ever since—to hear "Ja, vi elsker" moves me to tears. I am transported back to that day of unparalleled jubilation when the five-year German occupation of Norway was at an end. At last!

After meeting my American husband, I left Norway as a young adult and settled in the United States. During all these decades since then, I have kept in touch with my Nordstrand grade school classmates, returning for multiple school reunions and bridging the distance per telephone in-between. The Nazis may have taken over our country during those five years of war, but never the soul of its people. The friendships formed so long ago under such adverse conditions proved to be lifelong, keeping me connected as well to my native language and culture for which I am boundlessly grateful.

THE LYSHAUG COLLABORATORS

by Elizabeth Lyshaug, David Bergey and Astri Grieg Fry

Tor Lyshaug grew up in the greater Oslo area, first in the Nordstrand's east side and later in the Slependen/Sandvika area to the west. He was only sixteen when two major events affected his life: the start of the German occupation in Norway, and the unexpected death of his father only two months earlier.

The family's second location provided a view of the Oslofjord clear down to the strategic narrows at Drøbak. Here the German heavy cruiser *Blücher* was sunk by Norwegian cannon fire on that fateful invasion date: 9 April, 1940. The family's back yard provided a ringside view of even more immediate action. From there, Tor watched enthralled as British and German fighter planes engaged in air battles. Once debris from the planes began to fall into the garden, however, he deemed it prudent to retreat indoors. Not much later into the war, a car stopped outside the Lyshaug residence one day and two German officers stepped out. They were planning to install anti-aircraft batteries, and they thought this location would be ideal. But the courageous Jenny firmly responded, "Nei!" and, surprisingly, the enemy backed down. Left with the property intact, Jenny grew potatoes and vegetables in her large garden to supplement the family's food supply. Her home also became a center for son Tor and his Resistance cohorts.

Early in the war, Jenny worked for the Rationing Authority Office in Sandvika which was controlled by the Germans. While there, she slipped extra coupons out to people who were in dire need of boots and winter clothing until she lost her job because she was not a Nazi. Prior to that event, Jenny had become a courier and passed vital information within the Norwegian Resistance Movement. This was a most risky undertaking. Nazi sympathizers could be anywhere, informing on one's activities or utterances. After losing her job, Jenny still had an income, albeit mysterious. Under her doormat month after month, there appeared a salary. It was enough to support this unemployed Resistance widow with two teenage children.

Jenny suspected that family connections in England may have stood behind this inexplicable benefaction which tided her over until she got a job with Oslo Sparebank in 1943. However, she was not the only courageous woman in the family. Her younger sister, Astrid Petersson, was married to a King's Guard officer. His initial participation in the war had been to order the extraction of German soldiers from the frigid Oslofjord waters as the *Blücher* sank. Nevertheless, since then, Aksel, an active-duty Norwegian military officer, had found it necessary to flee to England. He had done so the long way around: via Sweden, Russia, the Far East and the United States. When Astrid later wanted to join him in England, she took a more direct but riskier route. She rowed a boat across a river between occupied Norway and neutral Sweden—solo—and in the middle of the night.

Meanwhile, young Tor, galled by the callousness universally displayed by the German invaders, began to fight back in his own way. While still in high school, he and two peers made a placard (since on display in Norway's Resistance Museum at Akershus, Oslo). It baldly stated the following: "NOTICE! The Valler School student who attends the NS meeting on Wednesday will be considered a traitor. He (she) will be treated as such! Whoever attempts to tear down or damage this notice will be beaten up!! [signed] S. S. U." It wasn't long before the school was shut down, and this placard may be have been a contributing factor. In his senior year, Tor attended classes held in private homes and graduated in 1943.

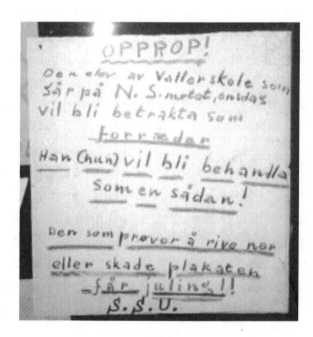

Once Tor began engaging in clandestine activities, it wasn't long before he attracted an adverse German interest. While he was eating dinner at home one day, suddenly three German officers appeared outside. Tor grabbed his coat and exited out the back door. Downhill from the back yard were railroad tracks. Tor raced through the vegetable patch and over to a friend's house on the other side of the tracks. Meanwhile, so as to preserve normal appearances during this intrusion, his grandmother quickly had sat down to Tor's unfinished meal while the Germans ransacked the entire house—fruitlessly.

Being small for his age, Tor was a natural candidate when he and some others crawled through a sewer drainpipe to place explosives under a local long and rectangular Gestapo Headquarters building. Once the explosives were ignited, the building then literally tipped over into the street. In retribution, the Germans lined up and machine-gunned the first fifty unsuspecting Norwegian pedestrians. This created a moral dilemma for Tor. It tormented him that Norwegians were gunned down as a result of the Gestapo HQ bombing. At the same time, he felt that the actions of the Resistance were necessary and in the long run would prevent deeper levels of abuse by the German troops.

Of vital importance to the German war effort was the supply of ball bearings for tank production. In Oslo there was such a factory, the Swedish-based SKF. During the war this was under German control until 4 December, 1944. Then Tor's group, dressed in the SKF workers' uniforms, entered the plant, hoisted two drums of gasoline up the elevator shaft of the building and ruptured them at the top of the shaft, filling the plant with fumes. Once they ignited the vapors, the resulting explosion completely destroyed the factory.

A similar effort targeted fuel tanks storing gas for the German military. These reservoirs had a capacity of up to 400,000 gallons. When the saboteurs ignited them, Tor observed that "the tops flew around like flying saucers."

Tor also joined *gutta på skauen*, the boys in the back country, aspiring soldiers who acquired military training in the Norwegian wilderness areas. Survival skills of this nature were critical by now. Tor knew he was wanted by the Gestapo during the latter two and a half years of the war. One guerrilla tactic employed by these troops was to string piano wire across forest roads. In the best case scenario, German soldiers roaring through on their motorcycles might part company with their heads. Perhaps more realistically, they might be ejected from their bikes, sprawled upon the ground and subject to further attack. Engagements such as this took their toll. One time when Jenny and Tor happened to be on the same subway train, the mother didn't even recognize her own son as he had grown so thin.

While the family still lived in Nordstrand, Tor had known some Jewish youngsters from well-to-do homes. His impression was that the Jews were well liked and respected for their good businesses in downtown Oslo. During the war, Tor helped some Norwegian Jews escape to

14

Sweden. Like the sabotage activities, this also was terribly risky, and it was extremely difficult to get the Jewish families to understand the danger they were in. They didn't want to believe the horrendous reports of the extermination camps that had begun circulating. When confronted by the Germans, they would admit to being Jewish, which didn't further their cause at all. One specific escape incident was hiding a group of Jews in a horse wagon's load of hay. The farmer driving the wagon didn't feel confident that his passengers would remain quiet, and exposure would have been dire for everyone concerned.

Despite the mandatory confiscation of the radios by the Germans starting early in the war, the Lyshaug family kept a radio in their attic. Tor's high school French teacher was of an austere and formal nature. He was generally attired in a black suit and had a trick of wearing his glasses far down his nose. Tor would listen to BBC broadcasts aimed at France and repeat the news to his waiting teacher. This performed wonders both for Tor's understanding of French as well as for mutual morale. When the German battleship, *Bismarck*, heading for the relative safety of occupied France was sunk by the Allies in 1941, however, the French teacher's habitual reserve evaporated completely. Tor was doubly pleased. In addition to sharing this exciting news with his teacher, his linguistic efforts had earned him an "A" in French.

Another significant battleship loss for the Germans was the *Tirpitz*, sunk in November 1944 with a great loss of life. Years later, in 1952, Tor, having meanwhile served in the Norwegian Air Force and now a civil engineer involved in dam building, had the opportunity to walk on its hull. The ship was still lying there in the Tromsøfjord.

When the war in Norway concluded by 8 May, 1945 with Allied help, Norwegians regained control of their own country. The Germans troops were deported to their homeland. When boarding a ship, each soldier was ordered to strip his uniform of insignia and open his luggage for inspection. One officer in particular refused to tear off his medals. Moreover, when he opened his bags, they were full of "war souvenirs" taken from a home, presumably one he had commandeered from a Norwegian family during the occupation. This irked his Norwegian inspector. When the German still balked and started berating him, the Norwegian, his patience exhausted, shot him dead on the spot. For Tor, this was an example of the arrogance that the Germans habitually displayed as their defining characteristic, and he never forgot this incident.

After marrying Elizabeth Anne Wilcox and residing permanently in the US from 1953 until he passed away in 2009, Tor continued to value his Norwegian roots and was a member of Sons of Norway's Grieg Lodge in Portland. One year he delivered the keynote Syttende Mai speech there, describing the clandestine wartime activities of both his mother and himself, with his mother and other family members present.

It was only after the five-year Nazi occupation of Norway that mother and son had learned of each other's involvement in the Norwegian Resistance Movement.

WAR MEMORIES

A letter by Jens Velken to his daughter, Sigrid Button;
translated by Anna Mosey

I have been asked to write about the early days of the war in 1940, and where I was and what I did during those days. When the war started, I was a corporal in the Fourth Guard Company in Oslo. The night of April 9, we were commanded to leave the barracks, given ammunition and then loaded onto Oslo city buses. We were driven directly to the town of Drøbak, where we stopped at a farm close by the Oslofjord. We could look down to the fjord where the German ship *Blücher* was visible; maybe it had hit a rock, or maybe the ship had been hit by torpedoes from the fort, we thought.

We were sent to the beach to capture German prisoners who had managed to get to shore. A friend and I accompanied some Germans to the farm, and I said to my friend that it was sad to see the Germans walk barefoot in the snow. One of the Germans answered in very good Norwegian that the distance to the farm is short, so the cold did not bother him. Another German climbed on top of a rock, made a fist in the direction of the fort and said: "If it had not been for that damned torpedo, I would have been director of the telegraph and telephone systems in Oslo now." I found a very nice briefcase on the beach, which I gave to one of the commanders. It was so fancy that we figured it belonged to a high-ranking officer. Wonder what the briefcase contained. The beach was very dirty and the

18

sea was full of diesel oil from the ship. There were many German casualties. It was as if dirty cabbage heads were sticking up from the ocean—a sight one does not forget so easily.

But then we received orders to get back to the Guard as fast as possible, because the commanders had learned that the Germans were surrounding us. In a hurry, we boarded the buses and left the prisoners. The Germans stopped us only once.

However, one day they almost got us. We were keeping watch in the hills above a valley where the Germans were stationed, when some of us received unexpected gunfire from behind. The Germans had climbed up the hill through a side valley. I was lying next to a buddy with a machine-gun when a hand grenade was thrown toward us from behind. It rolled under a fence, but did not go off. My buddy threw himself around and emptied the magazine into a snow bank close by. That was the end of those who were hidden in the bank. Somewhere a German was still threatening us when I saw an eye looking out of a window in an outhouse, and the next thing we knew, both the German and the outhouse were annihilated. German planes flew over and dropped bombs on us and they could see the machine gun fire from the plane. I threw myself under the branches of a pine tree and held onto a branch, but then a rain of bullets cut off the branch. Many of my friends lost their lives that day. We received orders to get out of that area if at all possible. A friend and I managed to climb higher up into the hills. After some time, some guards and commanders arrived on horseback, but they belonged to another company. Up to this point, they had moved only at night and taken position against the Germans through the hills during the day until evening. One night, we were going to rest in a shed and we were preparing our "bed" out of hay, but when I got an attack of hay fever, I decided in a hurry that I wanted to stand guard outside all night.

If I had told anybody during times of peace that I went for a whole week without sleep, they would have called me a liar, but in war much is possible. We had a lieutenant in the Guard Company who looked like a general with straight back and neck. Then the war came and he fell apart like a child. I think he was discharged from the military.

In the Guard, we had a sergeant that we teased a bit. He was small and thin and it seemed that his voice was still changing. Still, in the war, he was one of the best soldiers I saw. He knew how to respond to the German attacks and he even gave orders. The company we belonged to liked to get our clean uniforms and our shiny shoes just like we did during peaceful times, and fortunately, he had a contact who did his best to help us out—he worked under second in command, Captain Odd Mølster, at Voss.

One day, we received orders to join a group of English troops, because they had been a fiasco. We were told that the first time they came under fire from the Germans, they ran away and abandoned their weapons and their defense position. We provided a good position for

20

them, which they left and retreated to the boats in Ålesund. On our own way back from the Front, we discovered on the ice at Lesjaskogvatnet (the Lesja Forest Lake) what was left of the Norwegian Air Force—a mere wreck. We drove past Åndalsnes toward Åfarsnes and found lodging on a farm. After the English left, the Germans arrived—some without their weapons. Not enough food, but one day, somebody got hold of a sack of rice. It was cooked in a kettle in *ildhuset,* a small house on old farms used for cooking and tool-making, and this was great as long as it lasted.

One day, a notice was posted that those who needed to go home to do the spring planting should sign up to do so. At once, there were rumors that this was a plot to get laborers for farms in Germany. I talked with Odd Mølster, who said that the notice was not a trick, so I signed up. After a few days, we received transportation to Oslo on the back of an open truck. We spent the night in a school in Lillehammer. I practically sat in the lap of the commander and the dust was terrible.

In Lillehammer, we got a classroom in a school the Germans had left. We still wore our Guard uniforms, and one of the German commandos asked our commando if we were part of the group who had been on the Front—the group that they had called "the Black Devils." We were amused by the praise.

When I arrived in Oslo, I went directly to Uncle Lars (City-Lars) because I needed a bath and some civilian clothes. Uncle Lars called Knut Lillegraven (?) to tell him that I had been found. One evening, I went to Arve's house —with Knut and their wives we enjoyed a dinner and pleasant companionship. During the dinner, he (Knut) told that on April 9, he had been on his way to his office and was stopped by a German officer, who asked for direction to some place. Knut started giving directions in German, but stopped abruptly, and told the German that he did not understand. The German grew angry and told Knut that he spoke German like a native. Knut enjoyed telling this story. It took a few days before I could travel west to Voss, and that trip took two days. I want to mention that Johan O. Kjerbond was in my troop in the Guard, but was on medical leave and did not join the war effort. Likewise, Prestegård in Ulvik was on guard duty that night, and could not join out troop.

Will mention that there are few events that are worth giving information about in the rest of my military service. When the peace came, I served as a guard at Eide to watch over the Germans who were on their way to Bømoen to be gathered up there. We had to be cautious because we suspected that they were in possession of a few guns still. Then I was recruited to join the Norwegian forces, which were then stationed at Liland Hotel. There had been five years without new commanders, and many were still abroad, so there was a shortage of commanding officers. I do not know how it happened that I became a troop leader, but that is how I served. But, after the good training that I had received in the Guard, I had no difficulties commanding or doing other things.

22

The boss of the forces at Voss was—as far as I can remember—Capt. Haukeland. He applied to I.R.10 for the West to promote two corporals commandos for the Guard because of good service, and I was one of those two corporals. This was denied, but I was offered admittance to Officers' training, but I did not accept.

When I arrived at Bømoen, I received a job as Postmaster for the troops at Voss. It was Tore Furuberg who recommended me to Capt. Haukeland. It was a good job with a 350.c.c. DKV motorcycle with good bags for the mail. So this was the last task I had in the military. What I have written is nothing to brag about, but it is nothing I am ashamed of either.

To be fair, I need to mention something I forgot earlier, something our commando had learned in conversation with an English commando. He shared that the English who had been promised as a help to Norway had no military training. And I believe this is true. I always had a good relationship with my commanders and was therefore informed of what was going on.

An afterthought, but I offer no solution. While growing up, I was always careful in my conduct and watched out for the danger. But then came service in the Guard and the war. Caution disappeared and if there was a request for voluntary service, I was usually there. Often this included scouting for German troops and reporting messages to our company. One time sergeant Vastor (?) and I were in a house that was being destroyed by German cannons. We managed to get to the cellar. We agreed that we would probably not survive, but did our best as long as we could. How can a person change so fast?

I heard in a lecture that it was said that when a person has served on the Front and survived, he will not be the same as before.

I thought little about that until something happened. Hulda and I were invited to a family reunion and the old people who were present there came from the Lofthus side of the fjord. After the dinner, some of us men were outside, and a man, or better said, a person, approached me and asked if I was from Norway, and I responded. Then he said I ought to be ashamed that I let the Germans take Norway without firing a shot. Norway was well prepared for guerrilla warfare and we had weapons, he said. I asked him to go to the library to borrow books from that era, but he did not give in. Then something happened that I do not quite understand. In my mind, I saw those soldiers who had died, and they asked for my help to speak up for them. I told this to the person, and as I spoke my words and expressed that, I wanted to grab him and throw him in the swimming pool nearby. I would have done this, but he ran away. I got hold of Hulda, found the host and said thank you. The host told me this person was Swedish and was married into the family, and they had difficulties with him.

How I could react so strongly after so many years is something I do not quite understand yet. It happened again later when a German, who had participated in the burning of Hammerfest, told how lucky we were that they had come to Norway to help us. I said a few well-chosen words and got out of there before I said or did something I ought not. Hulda says it took a couple of weeks before I calmed down. I write about this because there is much I do not understand.

JOURNEY OF DEATH

Exhibit, Norway's Resistance Museum at Akershus, Oslo;
submitted by Ron Petersen

We suspected doom
that last evening ashore.

This was the way it always was
before the convoy set sail.
There was comfort in spirits
when the world could come to an end tomorrow
or in four days.

Loud laughter and strong words
in English, Norwegian and other languages
disappeared in the smoke and dim light,
as we pulled a girl close
dancing by the table
and during the night.

A NORWEGIAN SEAFARING FAMILY THROUGHOUT TWO WORLD WARS
by Hans Teisner and Astri Grieg Fry

The family stories I, Hans Teisner, have to relate are inextricably linked to the sea and Norway as a seafaring nation. My maternal grandfather, Einar Teisner, initially sailed on sailing ships in the Far East. Later he sailed on the North Sea route, and during this time, World War I broke out.

Despite Norway maintaining a neutral position during the first World War, several thousand seamen lost their lives onboard ships which transported supplies to the Allies. Our merchant fleet, then as now, ranked as one of the largest in the world, and the wartime shipowners reaped immense profits.

Einar Teisner served onboard the *SS Borgsten I*, which in 1917 was torpedoed by a German submarine UC64 in the English Channel. Einar, who was a chief engineer (allegedly the first chief engineer onboard this ship), clambered, along with other crew members, into the lifeboats. His lifeboat was still attached to the sinking ship, but fortunately he had a knife along and thus was able to sever the rope and release the lifeboat from the ship. All aboard were rescued later.

Both my father, Paul Arthur Johansen and his brother, Hans Adolf Johansen, attended the Horten Technical School and became chief engineers by the age of twenty-five.

During World War I, Arthur sailed with the Navy and was stationed at Oscarsborg. He served aboard a warship which patrolled the Oslofjord, participating in protecting Norway's neutral waters. In 1922 the *SS Borgsten II* was employed in the North Sea service, until it was sold in 1957. Arthur was the last chief engineer aboard this ship.

Prior to the onset of World War II, Arthur sailed between Europe and the US west coast, the Pacific Line, on various Fred. Olsen & Co. vessels. On 28 December, 1939, Arthur signed on with the *MS Knute Nelson*. Once World War II broke out, however, all Norwegian ships in international waters were ordered to return to Norway's harbors by the Germans. Fred. Olsen records show that on 9 April, 1940, the *MS Knute Nelson* sailed into German controlled waters in the Oslofjord. En route, the crew observed several bodies floating in the sea. These were Norwegian casualties from a Coast Guard vessel which had gone down after encountering the invading German fleet earlier that day. Arriving in Fredrikstad, the cargo of the *MS Knute Nelson* was unloaded and the crew discharged.

By the autumn of 1940, the *MS Knute Nelson* had been absorbed into *hjemmeflåten*, the Home Fleet, now under German control. However, by now there was no ignoring the perils of wartime sea service. According to Norwegian Home Fleet records, already a year before, on 3 September, 1939, the British passenger ship *SS Athenia* was torpedoed northwest of Ireland by the Germans. The *MS*

Knute Nelson rescued 449 survivors, with other ships also arriving to assist at the scene. Despite such risks, Arthur applied for the position of chief engineer when the *MS Knute Nelson's* new crew was signed on in September 1940, but he was not reinstated. The position went instead to Chief Engineer Rangvald Kristoffersen on 15 September, 1940, a man with some influence within the Fred. Olsen company. Kristoffersen died when the *MS Knute Nelson* was sunk by the Allies off Jæren in Western Norway on 27 September, 1944.

On my wife Vivian's side of the family, as the Norwegian Sailors' Memorial Hall records show, a distant relation became yet another war casualty. Captain of the *SS Erviken* (leaving behind his wife and their two children), Paul Johan Heesch died on 16 October 1941 when the *SS Erviken* was crossing the Atlantic in convoy. Several German submarines attacked and the *SS Erviken* sank immediately along with 25 men, although 14 others of its crew did survive.

Whether or not there was a war on back then, being a seaman was hardly the easiest career choice. Ship captains had the means to buy shares in their shipping companies as a way of securing their jobs. Thus they could take some time off and know they had a position to return to. For others at sea, however, possibilities were considerably more limited. My uncle Hans, for example, at one point sailed as chief engineer for ten years at a stretch with no vacation. This is quite a statement about the maritime working conditions of yesteryear!

In a seafaring family such as mine, the husband's absence for prolonged periods was simply a way of life. Now Arthur, however, having been bypassed for further wartime service aboard the ill-fated *MS Knute Nelson*, uncharacteristically was at home over a longer period. For the remainder of the war, he held several temporary jobs. First he became the director of a *knottefabrikk*, a wood chip factory, in Østerdalen. *Knott*, small wooden chips, were used as fuel and a supplement to the gas in cars. A boiler was mounted to the back of a vehicle, the wood chips were burned, the water in the boiler heated, and the car was drivable under its own steam, as it were, although hardly operable at any great speed. Later on during the war, Arthur found employment in the Bundefjord as a shipyard watchman.

Both Arthur and my mother Einarda, daughter of Einar, owned property on an Oslofjord island, Killingholmen, and perhaps this was how they met each other. They were married in 1941, and I, Hans, and my twin sister, Grethe, were born in 1942.

At Killingholmen during the war, some rural properties, such as my family's, were large enough to sustain the cultivation of vegetables and potatoes, keeping poultry, and there were some cattle on the neighboring island. The local fish market supplied the regional inhabitants with fish and other seafood, and during a time of rationing cards and very limited access to fresh produce in a northern climate, this must have been a vital and most welcome supplement.

OLAV BRAKSTAD: STUDENT YEARS ARRESTED

by Erik Brakstad and Astri Grieg Fry

Although my father, Olav Brakstad, experienced World War II in Norway, it was not something he enjoyed talking about. Nevertheless, he understood that people were interested, and became more willing to talk about his wartime experiences later in life.

Olav was eighteen years old and in his last year of *gymnas,* high school, when the war came to Norway. He lived in Eidsvoll, a small city about an hour north of Oslo. He was looking forward to his *russetid,* that carefree and celebratory interval between final exams and graduation, and had been elected editor of his school's *russeavis,* the senior newspaper.

Although political tension in Europe had been mounting, Norway was committed to maintaining a position of neutrality that had served it well during the first World War. However, the Germans struck with a well-coordinated attack on April 9, 1940 and occupied Norway for five long years.

Olav thought the early days of the occupation were somewhat exciting. Norwegian government officials fled north through Eidsvoll, and briefly used his *gymnas* as a meeting space. Then the Germans came and used it as barracks and a field hospital for casualties from skirmishes in the area. Olav and a friend photographed themselves by the wreckage of the nearby Minnesund bridge that had been blown up by Norwegian forces as they tried to slow down the Germans' northward progress.

Freedom of speech was repressed: Syttende Mai celebrations were banned. The possession of radios was declared illegal and all were to be turned in to the authorities. Nevertheless, a neighboring farmer kept a radio hidden in his chicken coop. Listening to nightly BBC broadcasts in Norwegian gave everyone a much better sense of what was going on in the world than they got from the Nazi-controlled propaganda. Broadcasts would often conclude with seemingly nonsensical phrases, which in reality were coded messages for the Norwegian Underground Movement.

With their twisted ideas of racial superiority, the Nazis thought Norwegians would fall into line as their natural Aryan allies. But they were so heavy-handed and tone deaf that they didn't win many Norwegian hearts and minds. Early in the occupation, the Germans staged a cross-country ski race in Eidsvoll to try to engage young people. It didn't work according to plan. The skiers came to a pre-arranged point in the course where they just stopped skiing. They stood in a group and sang patriotic songs, and the competition simply had to be called off. One time my father saw a German soldier plodding along on skis, getting ready to try to ski down a hill with a tricky spot at the bottom. Norwegians, after all, learn to ski almost as soon as they are able to toddle around, and it was highly amusing when members of the "master race" attempted to ski. Olav had his camera and hid out at the bottom of the hill. When the German soldier crashed, as expected, Olav popped out —"CLICK!"—and darted off. Fortunately the soldier was unarmed, but the frosty air was filled with obscenities that extended far beyond Olav's high school knowledge of the German language.

By 1943, Olav was an Oslo University student. One day that November, he was studying in the library and a warning note was passed from hand to hand saying that the Germans were coming. But there had been so many rumors before that the students hardly knew what to believe. The mood in the library became restless and loud, and Olav decided to leave. He looked out of the window and saw that German soldiers had surrounded the building. He ran out the back door and scaled the fence, but a soldier poked a rifle at him and he gave himself up. He and over 1000 other students were initially sent to Larvik, and were interned in a dirty building that had previously housed Russian prisoners. Olav didn't take the situation that seriously at first, until he realized they were to be shipped off to Germany. He was subjected to a "selection process." Fortunately for him, however, he had a stomach flu, so he was not allowed on the ship to Germany.

Olav was eventually sent to Grini, Norway's largest concentration camp to the northwest of Oslo, where he was assigned prisoner number 9446. On his first day there, an "old-timer" with only a three-digit number, gave him the inside scoop: "Be careful what you say to any stranger; one out of ten prisoners here is an informer." This was a prime example of the Germans being masters of the divide-and-rule tactic. While Grini was not like the horrendous death camps in central Europe, being incarcerated there was no picnic either. Observation and proximity quickly revealed the caliber of the prison guards. They represented the dregs of the German military; those who were not considered worthy of serving at the Front.

In Grini, food rationing followed a lottery system in each barrack. The allotted potatoes were lined up in as equal rows as possible, with numbers alongside and the drawing would match a bunk number. If one's row of potatoes seemed somehow unequal, there would be highly controversial reactions by the famished inmates. Prisoners worked from 7:00 a.m. to 6:00 p.m., with a one hour break at noon for dinner. Once an inmate got creative by getting hold of a dead crow, which he cooked and pronounced delicious eating.

Three times a day the prisoners marched out for roll call. They had little free time to call their own. In the evening, surreptitious activities were organized with musical instruments or lectures. One of the university professor prisoners had been able to obtain the French book of plays that was with Olav when he was arrested. He and Olav found solace in reading the plays to each other. While diverting themselves at these rare intervals, the inmates would post their own sentry to alert them of an approaching guard so that everything would appear "normal" by the time a Nazi inspector arrived.

The prisoners' response to their enforced labor was to practice passive resistance. That is, doing as little as possible the moment the guards turned their backs: "The danger is over, stop pretending to work!"

In the barracks, the inmates were crammed together, with rows of three bunks stacked on top of one another. When the prisoners were to be punished, the guards made them perform pushups in the slush and mud, a practice called *hinlegen*. Olav once saw an older man in his forties who collapsed and died as a result of this punishment.

In 1942 my grandfather, Edvard, was sent to a prison camp in Kirkenes in Northern Norway for his role in the nationwide teachers' resistance to the Nazification of the schools. In 1944 my uncle by marriage, Ole Petter, was arrested and sent to a horrific camp called Stutthof in Poland where, as he recounted later, "he should have died many times over." Given this contrast with his brother-in-law's grueling ordeal, Olav felt that he didn't have much right to complain about his own prison camp stay. The worst part for Olav, as it was for his father in Kirkenes, was the constant hunger and the absolute uncertainty of what was going to happen. On December 23, 1944, however, Olav was unexpectedly released and was able to make it home for Christmas. Once there, he annoyed his family by continuing the prison camp practice of knocking at every door to signal that he wasn't in fact a German.

As the war was still on, Olav went to work for a farmer to avoid having to do compulsory work for the Germans. Not long after he had returned home, he was asked to join the Norwegian Resistance, and he accepted.

Norwegian Home Front soldiers, Olav Brakstad on left

At one point he was tasked with transporting a typewriter (considered contraband like radios, they could be used to produce Underground newsletters). His solution was to balance it on his bicycle handlebars and, when passing a German police station, assume an expression of utter boredom and nonchalance.

Although weapons weren't really his thing, Olav was issued a US Carbine and brandished that, along with wearing a makeshift uniform, on May 8, 1945—the day the Germans capitulated. There was a German stronghold outside of Eidsvoll, and he was asked to be the interpreter representing local forces as they accepted the German surrender. While the Germans still were armed to the teeth, they were tired of the war and were good at following orders. They surrendered without incident.

Later that spring Olav had the opportunity to work with British "Red Devil" paratroopers who had the dual assignment of improving existing maps of Norway and searching out remaining Gestapo members who were trying to pass themselves off as "only Wehrmacht" soldiers. Olav was fascinated by these British paratroopers—they had suffered tremendous casualties in *Operation Market Garden* the previous autumn, with many having been killed or taken prisoner. This left the majority of the survivors utterly reckless and fatalistic.

After the war, Olav resumed his studies at the University of Oslo. In 1947 he was an exchange student in Iowa for a year—one of the best years of his life. Upon his return to Norway, he obtained advanced degrees in both psychology and French. He met and married an American woman, Cynthia, and they married in 1954. Later that year they moved to the US and bounced around the West Coast before settling in Bremerton, Washington, where he was an instructor of psychology at Olympic Community College.

In retirement, Olav put together a booklet which contained his wartime photographs and story. He made it available online, and would occasionally speak in public. ("Although wouldn't they rather see pictures from my latest trip to Norway?") His last public appearance was on May 12, 2000 at Portland State University at the Scandinavian Heritage Foundation's Friday Night Lecture Series. The lecture hall was packed, and he captivated the audience with his matter-of-fact and unassuming manner. He didn't take the opportunity to make himself look heroic, nor did he demonize Germans. He simply told his story so that the rest of us could have a inkling of what those difficult war years were like.

THE DIARY OF EDVARD BRAKSTAD
by Olav Brakstad

A translation of two letters and parts of a diary written by my father, Edvard Brakstad, during captivity in 1942. Some explanations are added.   *June 16, 2011*

Unloading a German ship at Kirkenes

Some historical background information:

Norway was invaded by Germany during the early morning hours of April 9, 1940. I was then an 18-year-old high school student and lived with my parents in Eidsvoll, 50 miles north of Oslo. We heard the news of the attack over the radio as we were getting up in the morning. It was a total surprise.

Over the news the day before we had heard that the British had laid mines along the Norwegian West coast, and we were disturbed by this breach of Norwegian neutrality by "our friends." Up to then, Norway had been engaged in a balancing act trying to remain strictly neutral so as not to give one or the other of the two warring powers an excuse to invade the country and make use of it against the other side. There was little doubt, however, that among the majority of Norwegians the sympathy was with the Allies. Some among us, who were especially well informed, had heard about German warships leaving their bases and moving up the Atlantic in a northerly direction. But it was believed that this was done in preparation for some action in the Atlantic, perhaps a major encounter with the British fleet there. My sister and I had our minds on things closer at hand: It was her 15th birthday that day, and we were busy celebrating it. Little did we know then that in less than two years first my father and then I would be sent off to German prison camps.

I remember running out in the snow before breakfast the next morning to get a look at the German planes high up in the sky. Later we saw flashes of light and smoke on the horizon as bombs were dropped in the Oslo area. We were all stunned, confusion reigned, and mobilization orders were issued too late to be effective in the southern part of the country. Norway had devoted most of her budget to social programs, very little to defense and was poorly prepared for war. However, at the old fort of Oscarsborg, situated at a narrow point of the Oslofjord, the shore batteries were activated, and the soldiers manning one of the ancient rusty cannons there managed to sink a heavy German cruiser, the *Blücher*. The Germans had not counted on this, and the sinking of the *Blücher* delayed the take over of Oslo long enough to enable the Norwegian King and the government to escape north to Elverum, with the Germans in hot pursuit, and eventually to England.

On the day of the invasion, we saw members of the Norwegian General Staff arrive at the Eidsvoll *Landsgymnas* (State High School) and use the buildings for a short meeting before they continued northward. Many of the officers eventually made it over to England as armed resistance was given up in Southern Norway. Smaller encounters between the Germans and scattered Norwegian groups continued to the north of us for a couple of days. Now the Germans occupied the high school. We saw trucks and later tanks heading north, some trucks returning with German corpses that were unloaded and stacked up in a school store room. I remember vividly walking by the store room looking through the window at these bodies with blown off faces and limbs, my first grim confrontation with the brutality of war.

When a friend and I a few days later drove about 20 miles north from where we lived, we could see partially buried German soldiers in the ditches along the road, a boot sticking out here, an arm there. We learned that Norwegian soldiers on skis, hidden by trees and bushes, had ambushed the advancing enemy troops, stopped them there until German reinforcements arrived, and then vanished unscathed in the woods. Fighting went on in the northern parts of the country where the Norwegians now were aided

42

by English and French expeditionary forces until the Allies withdrew from Narvik on the 8th of June.

In the evening of the day of the invasion, Vidkun Quisling, the leader ("Führer") of the Norwegian Nazi Party, *Nasjonal Samling* (in the following pages referred to as *N.S.*), announced over the radio that he had established a new Norwegian government under his command with the support of the German occupation forces, and that the present government was to be ousted. This act of treason on the part of Quisling served as a wake up call to the people and little by little galvanized the overwhelming majority in our resistance to the German invaders and Quisling's followers, the Quislings, as we called them.

It was of extreme importance that the King and the government managed to escape to London and carry on the war in exile. The Nazis took control of broadcasting and newspapers, dissolved all unions and organizations, and eventually confiscated our radios. Listening to the radio or being in possession of one became punishable by imprisonment or worse. Our "underground" contact with London through "illegal" radios and news bulletins we typed and passed from hand to hand was dangerous, but it was a link to the free world that provided us with information, moral and material support, and guidance in our resistance throughout the five years of occupation.

At first the Germans tried to win over the civilian population with propaganda: They were there to help us against the English-Jewish-Capitalist oppressors, we Norwegians were part of the pure Aryan race and should fight with them against the common enemy, etc. A couple of days after the invasion a friend of mine and I got into a discussion with a German soldier who was posted as a guard close to our driveway. We told him in our school German that we did not believe what he was trying to tell us. (The German soldiers all used the same phrases, often word for word. They obviously had been thoroughly drilled and brainwashed.) At one point my friend shouted: "Hitler ist toll! Hitler ist toll!" (Hitler is crazy) The soldier looked aghast. I was a little concerned for my friend, but nothing happened: The front between the occupier and the occupied had not hardened yet. A few months later it took less than that to be arrested, and gradually what we referred to as the "ice front" developed. We would not speak to any German, not even look at one or acknowledge a German's presence unless forced to do so. For some months during the first year of the occupation the Germans requisitioned a room in our house for an officer. He was a polite, friendly and well educated man, but no one in our house engaged in any conversation with him. By that time the "ice front " had taken hold. We wanted to make our uninvited "guests" feel very unwelcome in our country.

Our new "leaders" made it gradually more and more clear that all public servants would not only have to cooperate with them, but also show a positive attitude towards Nazi ideology and the New Order in Europe, of which Norway now was to become a part. They realized that to "re-educate " the nation it was of crucial importance to get control over school administrators and teachers and reform the entire educational system from kindergarten up to the university level. Early in the fall of 1940 the new Minister of Education prepared a circular to all teachers which contained a declaration of loyalty to be signed. In this declaration the teacher was to promise that he would instruct his students in the Nazi ideology and that he was to do his utmost to influence them to become believers in the *New Political Order*. Now more than ever, the letter said, it is true that whoever is not for us, is against us. Furthermore, it said, a teacher who does not wholeheartedly, in his private life as well as in his career, live up to this declaration, must immediately resign from his position. 12 000 copies were printed of this letter, and it was to be mailed out to every teacher in the country.

However, someone in the print shop saw to it that a copy of the circular got into the hands of the leaders of the still operative teacher union. They quickly composed a model letter for the teachers to use as an answer to the Quisling government, in which they stated that they now, as before, would be guided in their teaching by their conscience and the principles they as teachers had committed themselves to follow. This letter was received by the teachers before the government's circular was in the mail. The government found out, however, how its plan had been thwarted and gave up mailing out the circular.

But the efforts to gain control over the educational system continued. Next, the Nazi government sent a letter to all civil servants, including teachers, requiring them to sign a declaration stating that they would actively promote the *New Order*. But the Quislings had no more luck with that than with their earlier threats.

Then they tried another strategy: A governmental office was established that would oversee the hiring and promotion of teachers and all other civil servants. All the organizations involved protested. Angry speeches by top Nazi leaders followed.

In the meantime, an underground network replacing the now "illegal" teachers' organization was set up with printing presses hidden in basements and an efficient messenger system by which the teachers could be contacted all over the country. This way everybody could be kept informed about what was going on. The teachers could put up a united front against the Nazi demands, and, which was very important, each individual teacher could be assured that if anything should happen to him in his resistance against the oppressors, his family would be taken care of financially through funds collected for that purpose. Through contact persons in the right places it was possible to keep track of planned moves in the enemy camp. Thus it became clear that the Nazis and their followers, after securing control of all professional and labor organizations, planned to establish a *Riksting* to take the place of the present *Storting* (Parliament). After that the German occupants would have some "legal" backing for taking full control of the country, signing a peace treaty with Germany and mobilizing Norwegian youth. As this became known among teachers and other civil servants, the will to resist grew even stronger.

In the fall of 1940 our high school was back in session. My father was teaching, and I was back in school as a student. But with all the turmoil around us it was difficult to concentrate on school work. As in most high schools, we had members of the *hird* attending classes. These were young Norwegian Nazis dressed in uniforms like their models in Germany. We luckily had few of these types in our classes, so they were not able to cause serious trouble, but in some larger schools, where they were more numerous, they could be very provocative, harassing both teachers and fellow students and disrupting classes. Overall, the students were united behind their teachers, backing them up in their resistance against Nazification of the schools. One of the most memorable examples of this was when the new Department of Education, in an attempt to win us over to their side, declared one day during the winter as a National Sports Day. Every student in high schools all over the country was to participate in cross country ski races. I remember how we all started out, moving very slowly, and after having completed most of the course, stopped on a large flat area a quarter of a mile from the finish line and just stood there singing patriotic songs and having a good time until the whole thing had to be called off.

While this was going on in the high schools, we heard through the underground news network about growing trouble on other fronts: Several university professors were arrested. The bishops protested against interference in church and school matters, and after an escalation of this conflict, the bishops were dismissed. Physicians protested. The members of the Supreme Court protested and later were dismissed. Then the whole country got involved in a letter campaign by parents protesting the efforts to Nazify their children, the threats against the teachers, and the suspension of the bishops. Everybody, whether a parent or not, took part, overwhelming the Quisling government with a deluge of letters.

In the beginning of 1942, a new letter was sent to the teachers: Salaries were to be withheld and not released until they signed a document stating that they would promote the *N.S.* agenda. Almost no teachers responded. Quisling and his cohorts were in a dilemma: They now had to crush the teachers' resistance once and for all or give up all hope of bringing Norway into the "New Europe."

On March 20th 1942 a mass arrest of teachers began. In our home we were worried about my father, but for over a week nothing happened. We were beginning to wonder if the Eidsvoll teachers had been forgotten. But not so. On April 1st a deputy sheriff came to our door. My father had a few minutes to pack some underwear, a toothbrush etc., and then he was marched off to the waiting car. We were trying to take it calmly, telling each other that they could not possibly detain all these teachers for very long. It turned out that they could. We did not hear a word from my father for a couple of months. The same day two of my father's colleagues, Harald Goksøyr and Bjarne Svare, were also arrested. These three had all been quite outspoken during the conflicts with the *N.S.* and the local principal, who was a Quisling sympathizer.

From underground newsletters and from occasional eyewitness reports we gathered that the teachers first had spent some time at Grini, Norway's largest German prison camp. From there they were transported by railroad in stock cars to an improvised prison camp, Jørstadmoen, north of Lillehammer. Finally they were crowded like sardines into boats at Trondheim and shipped to Kirkenes as far north as you can travel by boat in Norway.

We learned later that both at Grini and at Jørstadmoen the Germans had tried to terrorize the teachers into submission. The Germans especially put the heat on during the transport to Jørstadmoen and the stay there. A dramatic and detailed report can be found in the book *Kirkenesferda* (The Kirkenes Experience) written by some of the ex-prisoners themselves. This book and various other reports tell how the teachers were packed into dark, cold stock cars. The sliding door on the side of the car was kept slightly ajar, the only possibility for relieving themselves while the train was underway. This was a problem for people with upset stomachs, which was a common reaction to the poor food. Once in a rare while the train would stop, the prisoners chased out and ordered to relieve themselves alongside the wheels or out in a field exposed to rain, snow, cold and wind while the Germans were shouting: "Quick! Quick! You have two minutes!" In *Kirkenesferda* one of the writers describes the bizarre, almost unreal, situation at Lillestrøm, where teachers and school administrators,

49

young and old, some with graying hair, were squatting on one side of the train and concerned onlookers lined up on the other in spite of the Germans' attempt to keep the transport a secret. At all the train stops crowds of people would appear cheering and singing the national anthem. Some had food packages for the teachers, most of which would disappear among the German guards. In some cases the guards would chase away people, among them children and elderly women, with the butts of their rifles. The bystanders shouted words of encouragement to the teachers, and school children would sing patriotic songs as the train slowly passed by. The support from the crowds all along the route was of tremendous help to the teachers in keeping their spirits up and strengthening them in their determination not to give in to their captors' demands.

The first transport from Grini stopped at Jørstadmoen about two in the morning. In typical German prison camp style, the prisoners got two minutes to get out of the stock cars, then line up and wait for an hour on the platform in front of the station. Too bad if they had not had time to get all of their baggage with them when rushing out of the railroad car.

Then in the light of lanterns from the pursuing trucks, with rifles pointed at them and harassed by the constant shouting of the guards, "Los!Los!"(Quick! Quick!), they were half walking, half running through the dark forest along a gravel road full of holes and mud piles, hungry, tired, some with a suitcase in hand. At about six in the morning they finally arrived at the Jørstadmoen prison

50

camp, and here they were kicked and shoved, screamed and shouted at to get into the barracks quickly, and as soon as the last one had managed to tumble inside, the door was slammed shut behind them. They stood crowded together in the dark. In each bed there was a sack with straw. They were too tired to pour the straw out, just collapsed on top of the sacks in the ice cold rooms.

"Gymnastics" in the slush at Jørstadmoen

The teachers had no clue why the Germans had brought them to Jørstadmoen, and they wondered for a while if their captors did. The premises had been drill grounds for the Norwegian military and were totally unfit to accommodate nearly 700 prisoners. It turned out, however, that they were to stay for 12 days, 12 days of nerve war and terror. The more or less improvised food was barely edible. The prisoners had to work outside without proper clothing and tools in rain and snow, do "exercises" where they had to crawl on their stomachs in the mud, and were knocked about and kicked by yelling guards. The rooms were not adequately heated, clothes could not be dried, etc. It became obvious that their captors saw it as their mission to make existence so miserable for the teachers that they would break down and sign the now famous declaration stating that they were willing to become members of the teachers *samband*, the *N.S.* controlled union. They were called in for individual interrogation and offered to be sent home if they would just sign. Only a small number did, some of whom were sick.

Eventually about 500 of the younger and healthier were picked out, sent north to Trondheim, and from there to Kirkenes, close to the Russian border, in the now notorious ship, the *Skjerstad*.

A place to sit and lie down was hard to find in the hold of the *Skjerstad*, and during the night, when it was covered, the air down below was terrible.

This boat was certified for 250 passengers, had life jackets for about that many, berths for about 100, and as far as food and wash room facilities were concerned, it was totally unfit to transport a group of nearly 500. The local shipping authorities, the captain, even a *N.S.* physician tried to persuade the Germans to stop this irresponsible undertaking, but to no avail. The teachers had to find some space wherever they could squeeze in. After all rooms were filled to capacity, they had to stand in corridors, in stairways, sit on boxes, barrels, and coils of rope. Worst off were those who were crowded into the hold, where they were packed together so tightly they could hardly turn around when lying down to sleep. The air down below was terrible, bathroom facilities scandalous, and there was no chance to escape in case of emergency. The food was bad and inadequate. The Red Cross tried to deliver food in some ports on the way, but most of these attempts were prevented by the Germans who in some cases would take the food for themselves. As if this were not bad enough, the waters along the coast were mined, and bombing attacks from Russian planes could always be expected. In the convoy in which they were going, the *Skjerstad* was lined up as a cover against Allied torpedoes for an ammunition ship sailing between it and the shore. The stop and go voyage lasted 17 days, and when the teachers arrived in Kirkenes on April 28th, they were exhausted and starved and many were sick. For further details see *Kirkenesferda*.

In the barracks the mice were lively during the night

A second contingent of teachers was shipped north from Grini a couple of weeks later. This group was smaller, 144 men, and the boat trip was therefore somewhat less harrowing. They arrived in Kirkenes with the *Finnmarken* on May 11th. The three Eidsvoll teachers, Goksøyr, Svare, and my father were in this group.

My father did not talk a lot about these things afterwards. They were not pleasant topics. And after it was all over, we were excited about the life in freedom ahead of us. But when I now read about the treatment the teachers went through in *Kirkenesferda*, it takes no stretch of imagination for me to believe it all. About one year after the arrest of the teachers I had the opportunity to become acquainted with Nazi prison camp methods myself when I was arrested with about a thousand other students.

My father's diary consists of notes he wrote with a pen or with a pencil on loose sheets of paper, most of it

54

quite legible. It was strictly "verboten" to write a diary, but the *Wehrmacht* (Army) soldiers who took over after the the *S.S.* (Nazi guards) at Kirkenes, did not keep a close eye on the prisoners' behavior inside their rooms, so a few of them took the chance of jotting down some notes. Much is left out, however, especially incidents of harassment, names, conversations and thoughts that would be compromising if discovered and read by the Germans. Also, he did not go into details about many of the common frustrations described in *Kirkenesferda*, such as working and sleeping in wet clothing, working double shifts without rest, being pestered by mice and rats, not receiving replacement for worn out clothing and shoes etc. With the diary as I find it now, are three letters, one of which was obviously never mailed. The other two arrived a couple of months after they were written.

Translation of the main parts of two letters:

Trondheim, April 30, 1942
Dear all three:

As you have probably heard, we are on our way northward. We don't know for how long. Things have been much better than one could expect where we come from. I am tanned and strong and have in many ways had experiences that I definitely wouldn't want to miss. Our spirits are high, and we are part of something big. The trip up the Gudbrandsdalen was in a way a unique experience, although we did not exactly travel first class. Now we are aboard a boat and are comfortable. *[There was more room on the second boat.]* Take everything calmly, keep your strength and belief, we are probably facing big changes and happier times. Take care of the garden and the house as best you can, and then we'll all do what we have to do, each in our place. I have had strength and peace of mind up to now, and I hope that will last. My companions are unusually fine people, many good old friends.

I cannot write more under these circumstances, because of regulations. Live well all of you, my thoughts again and again go to you.

Hopefully we'll meet again before too long. So now I get a chance to see North Norway after all! The weather here is beautiful. Our neighbors ask me to send their greetings.
All my love, Father.

P.S. Write as wisely as you can to mother about this, Ågot. Now one of the fellows is giving a lecture about North Norway. We are in the big first class dining room. *[To pass time and to keep their spirits up they took turns giving lectures on a variety of topics, when the guards were out of ear shot, because this too, naturally, was "verboten."]*

Olav, don't hesitate to ask the neighbors for advice about house and garden.

And do not worry about me, I have never taken part in anything bigger, and you are as much part of this as I am.

Elvenes at Kirkenes, June 7, 1942.
Dear all three,

We arrived here the 11th of May, live in barracks, 14 men in my room. Great guys all of them. We managed the trip well, good weather, interesting to see North-Norway. It has been cold so far. But I have been healthy the whole time and have managed everything quite well. Work outside, usually road work and other outdoor work.

Elvenes is about 9 km. from Kirkenes. Was at the Finnish border one day. Time passes quickly. Things are all right. You need not worry about me. Hope we will be released some time during the summer. What is uppermost in our minds, is the concern for you back home. Be calm, we will meet again before long.

Greet friends. Write clearly and only about things that concern us. With all my love,
Edvard

[In addition to road work in the area, the prisoners unloaded ammunition at the docks in Kirkenes. The ships and docks were bombed from time to time and this was the most hazardous work they did.

The first entry we find in the diary:]

May 24, 1942.
"Gray weather and slush. 60-70 horses outside our barracks; they came from Finland. Stomping and noise, muddy all around us, not very pleasant here today. Woke up

early: Up around 6 AM. One group went out to work at Kirkenes."

[In the evening a small choir came over from other barracks to sing in their hallway. It was my mother's birthday that day. He writes:]
"My thoughts go home. – Her birthday and all the memories from her birthdays. The children and everything that goes with the home. It was not easy to get through this day."

May 25.
"Milder weather. The horses have gone. A big drinking party in the German barracks next to us. A quiet day for most of us, but work for some at Kirkenes. The biggest thing that happened was a letter read aloud, from our leaders in Oslo *[Illegal letter from the underground leaders, smuggled in].*
Main points:

- They are following closely what is happening to us.
- Our families get all the financial help they need.
- 663 clergymen have resigned. 70,000 civil servants have written protests against the *samband.*
- The schools, for the most part, are in session although the teachers have not signed the loyalty pledge.
- Plans for the *Riksting* [New Parliament] will be dropped. Youth mobilization also dropped. Teachers' *samband* probably also dropped.

58

- There is 'feverish' activity to secure our freedom.
- People are praying for our safety.

The letter caused a quiet optimism amongst us. It is a common belief that we might be let free fairly soon. Our action has brought about big results."

May 29.

"No big happenings these days. The weather has been good for the most part. This evening a nice and mild wind. People think that we will be free soon – maybe as soon as the first of June. I think we must be prepared for a longer stay here. Yesterday there were air raid alarms and bombing in Kirkenes - today also. I am going to Kirkenes tomorrow to work at 6:30 AM- just about everybody's going. Nesse tried to steal sausages from the Germans, was caught and beaten up. The *Hauptman* [commander] gave a speech at roll call about it. It is a shame the way this is handled."

May 31.

"Yesterday I did unloading, working for the first time on the ship *Hallingdal.* Unloaded gasoline and oil for the *Wehrmacht.* Relatively easy work. I got some fish for dinner, some flatbread and a couple of cups of soup. Last night was a beautiful night. The sun was streaming in on my bed at 2:15 in the morning. Two or three times during the night there was bombing close to where the teachers were in Kirkenes. Yesterday there was a short air raid alarm. We had to stop working for a while - we saw

Russian planes up high. Antiaircraft guns were shooting. We took it calmly - one gets used to everything.

Yesterday and today there have been many rumors circulating, particularly about the trip home. Some think that we're going home tomorrow. Not very likely. I have talked to the others about being prepared for the worst, that we'll be here most of the summer, but the wish to go home is strong.

A quiet Sunday today, fine weather - spring is here. The leaves are getting ready to come out. Wind from the south, with rain at night and sun during the day.

I have been homesick today. Not much food - a very sparse dinner - a piece of fish and some soup. I have lost 2 kg. since we came here. I always feel hungry and weak."

[In following entries rumors about the trip home is a recurring theme. Because of the inadequate diet preoccupation with food increases. This in addition to the constant uncertainty and tension, make people a little irritable:]

[Date?]
"There will be minor bickering once in a while. We're all a little petty, and that is seen sometimes. Grabbing things for yourself is a strong drive in people, just as in animals. Food and concern for food is deep-seated, and it is hard to keep these drives within decent limits."

[The residents of Kirkenes continue to help them with or without permission from the guards.]

"Yesterday evening we were given a salmon, and everyone got a piece. It tasted wonderful."

[Help from local people improves the food situation:]

"Enough marmalade, canned goods, sausage, sugar, and liver paste. There is quite often herring. But in spite of this we seldom feel we've had enough."

[In the middle of June they move into tents. The weather is good for a while, and that helps the spirits.]

[Date?]

"Great weather the past two days. Yesterday morning I got up at 5, sunned myself and washed my entire body, got coffee, and had breakfast. A magnificent morning. It is amazing how fast things can change here in the north. Now it is full summer, and the leaves are almost fully grown. We have stayed around the tents and sunned ourselves. This really is just vacation living! So far, we like it better here than in the barracks; as long as the good weather holds, we are alright. Steady work yesterday, and good food, and good news *[doesn't say what kind of news, probably about the war]*. We wish the war would get to an end soon. Last night I woke up people in the tent at 11:30; the sky was clear and the sun was as bright as during the day. Many got up and we climbed up on a hill and stood there, very moved, for a half hour. A wonderful sight. --- But just a few kilometers from us people are killing each other."

June 24. Jonsok [Midsummer Day]

"Bright sunshine. Work has gone well. Road work. Dinner was good. Fish and soup. I felt almost full. Afterwards I sunned myself, long and well - naked. The weather was mild, like southern Norway at this time. The evening meal was good, and I felt as if I almost had enough. One and a half herring, plus herring paste and marmalade. Chewed down some powdered sugar afterwards; that helped fill us up.

At roll call, it was announced that our colleagues at Kirkenes camp are going to move up here. They will work on the airfield, 320 men. In all, 390 men are needed. We will fill in the gaps. Not pleasant to think about. The rest of us will work on the roads. When that became known, many were rather discouraged. But I don't think this change has anything to do with what time we will be let free. It is *Jonsok* and High Summer in Norway - memories and feelings come streaming on. Thoughts about those at home, and sadness that summer is passing while we're here in captivity - the summer we have dreamed about during the long, cold winter. Now the best of it will pass while we are separated from our home and our loved ones. But we pull ourselves together and keep calm. We are fighting for our people and for our freedom, our country and our children. For humanity. And we're hoping for better times. I hope things are going well back home. So I live with the hope that I will see my family before very long. We can stay up until 10 this evening. We might go out to see the midnight sun tonight."

[Date?]

"*Jonsok* evening was outstanding, clear and beautiful. Almost everybody in our tent came out. The sun remained for some time above the hill to the north. A strange atmosphere. An unusually beautiful color tone over the sky and the countryside. The lakes and the fjord were a very strong blue, the leaves and the grass intensely green. A melancholy feeling possessed us. We sang, quietly, a couple of verses of our national anthem, and then we had to go back to our tents and captivity again.

Jonsok Day [the next day] was also exceedingly beautiful. Work was not hard, pleasantly warm, around 25 degrees."[Approx. 75 degrees F]. But all of a sudden cold weather set in, with a north wind and rain, and then it is unpleasant to live in paper houses."

July 6.

"Grey and blustery weather. Work on the road was pretty easy. And it was a big day! Three letters today, and one yesterday, from Ågot. They were old, but wonderful to receive. Homesickness really takes hold of me. My thoughts focus on home and freedom. But we do have the strength to hold out. Rumors keep circulating, especially about the trip home, and we wish they would become reality."

[Date?]

"Weather good. Sunny and warm days. I work on the road, hard work, and a lot of shouting and harassment. Extremely unpleasant atmosphere, but we take it calmly."

July 15.

"This day too passed without anything happening as far as the trip home is concerned. It is as uncertain as ever. We had hoped that this would be the day of return. Now we hope that something will happen before the 31st. Some think it is going to be the 20th. It came like a cold shower for many when it was announced at roll call that the sick people would be picked out and sent home soon. But only the sick ones. An application was sent for the rest to be included. As I see it, nothing really has changed as far as our situation is concerned."

July 17.

"A gray and cold day. It is strange how quickly the weather changes here. It looks like it is getting a little brighter again, and that is good. People are feeling that the return trip is going to take place soon. I am not so sure that we have much foundation for that belief, but we can hope. Lists have been made with the names of the sick people here and the oldest, and it is said that they are going to return first. But most people feel that we will all be sent at the same time. We have to take it calmly and be patient.

Svare, Goksøyr and I got a pack of cigarettes each from Dr. Punterwald in Kirkenes today. That was the first pack of cigarettes I've had since I came north. As far as the food is concerned, it is just barely enough. I often feel weak and listless, but I think that my weight is holding up fairly well. We received some oatmeal today, and we made porridge. Tasted wonderful. We had a free day and rested well. But despite that felt weak this evening.

I should have mentioned before that a piece of shrapnel landed close to the tent a couple of days ago during an air raid, and the same day there was a rather intense bombing of Kirkenes. The house belonging to relatives of Fagerjord's [a fellow prisoner] was blown away. A lot of damage was done to German storehouses, ammunition depots and workshops. It was said that 60 German soldiers were killed and two civilians injured. So we are up in the front line now. Some of the teachers were inside the storehouse that was bombed, but fortunately none of them were injured."

[There is a pause of several days in his writing because of illness. The following entry is undated:]
"This is the first real illness I've had on this 'vacation trip'. I got it on Sunday the 19th, suddenly and severely, with very strong pain in my stomach and severe diarrhea. I was lying in the heather twisting and turning like a snake. Monday I was a little better, but didn't eat. In spite of my better judgement, I ate a little bit Tuesday and for awhile thought I was cured. What I had was a piece of herring, and then it started again. I got a high fever Wednesday and some very uncomfortable days and nights followed. A big

bright spot in all of this was a letter from Ågot Monday night. A wonderful little letter with only good news. I really feel how much I love her and the children and my home, and now, here in captivity, I can see how I did not fully value and appreciate the times we could share and be together, working so hard all the time and not really appreciating the good things in life. And I feel now that I will and can be a better human being after this. I feel sympathy with everybody who is suffering, everybody who is a prisoner or a soldier, and there are many of them, who are in the war against their own will. My sympathy for suffering people increases. Their lives are as valuable as ours, and I experience a feeling of rebellion stronger than ever against the insanity of war.

Yesterday Svare brought a telegram from Schjøt-Iversen [chief physician at the hospital in Eidsvoll], good news. There was an interesting little sentence that we interpreted a certain way [private "code"]. He says: "Orvald og Åse til Oslo til høsten". We interpret that as meaning: In the fall, things are going to normalize. Our children will go to the University of Oslo, and everything will be OK. Well, we will wait and see."

[Dates are hard to determine for the entries below]:
"On July 26 I was at an anniversary party [birthday] for Svare. Pleasant, and there were speeches. I gave a speech, Goksøyr also, and Svare responded with a speech. Much praise was expressed for Svare. As a present I gave him a

66

slice of bread, one cigarette, and a wooden knife. *[A letter opener. He did some wood carving with his pocket knife].* The doctor told me today that I had an inflammation of the colon, and we will just have to hope that it passes soon. If I only could get home, then everything would be fine."

"Yesterday was another Sunday. I spent the whole day in my sleeping bag with a fever, didn't eat anything. Had a strong pain in my stomach during the night, and it all came from the inflammation of the colon. The pills that you sent along with me, Ågot, helped a great deal. *[He seems to have his wife in mind here as a future reader of the diary].* Sunday morning the pain was almost gone and the following day also better. Spirits were pretty high in the tent, in spite of the fact that several people had stomach problems. One had the flu, and three patients had been sent up here from the group in Kirkenes. So today only three people from here were out working."

"We have to remember the great task we are accomplishing by being here, doing something for the cause that we think is right and is the reason why we are here. So we just have to take what comes and hope that this isn't going to last too long. Many prisoners have suffered more than we do, and soldiers on the Fronts, in many ways, are worse off than we. Our lives are not more valuable than theirs. There are so many who have made greater sacrifices in this horrible war.

Well, July is almost over, and if we are going to go home before school starts, it will have to happen soon. There will therefore be a lot of excitement here from now until the end of July and the first days of August. According to rumors, Dr. Palmstrøm has said as his personal opinion, that we are going to leave around the first of August.

I just got back from the doctor. I got a new kind of tablet and was assigned to light work. I still feel pain in my colon, but now only on one side, so there has been improvement. I have to keep my spirits up and think that things are going to get better, but it is not so easy to cure a stomach ailment when all you get to eat is very heavy bread, salted fish, and *spekesild* [preserved herring]."

July 30:
"This was an important day. It looks like the trip home might finally become a reality. There has been a lot of stir and upheaval in many ways. But then at roll call, the names of about 100 people were read, and they were supposed to be sent home in the first round. I was among them, but I really don't trust that this is going to happen and won't believe it until I'm told to start packing. But overall people take this calmly. Those who are to be sent first, are the ones who are ill and unable to work, and among these, the older ones. How they are going to travel, we don't know. Everything is still uncertain, but it looks like there will be a resolution soon."

August 2.

"New month. Our stay here has lasted longer than most of us had expected. Now summer is on its way out, and we are still sitting here. We haven't heard much about our return trip. Nothing more about the lists that the doctor has put together.

Improvement slow as far as my illness is concerned. It is two weeks now since I got ill. I'm a little better today, but feel weak, and my stomach is not well. I had some soup yesterday, and that was beneficial. Saved half of it for today, and got another portion through trading. One has to try to make use of all the possible means here when it comes to diet. We've been thinking a lot about home today, and for me it probably has something to do with my illness. All this uncertainty here is hard on all of us. Yesterday it was said that schools in Oslo are going to start on September 1st. And most of us take that as a good sign. Otherwise spirits are rather low around here, even among those that were mentioned on the list for early departure."

[Early part of August]

"Important things have happened the past few days. I am almost well now after this terrible stomach illness, but I feel weak. I have some appetite, sometimes a little too much appetite, and I have been working several days.

Tuesday it was said that we who were going home, had to sign a declaration stating that we would become members of the teachers' *samband* after recovery from our illness and that we would resume our school work. There was a

69

big discussion about this. It was said that there would be an addition to the paper, stating that if one of the group refused to sign, that would affect all of us. But it turned out that this latter part was not correct. Overall there was an agreement to go along with this demand, but many harsh words were said during the discussion of the matter, and many had a tendency to bring up accusations against their friends: It was out of consideration for the old, sick and feeble that they now would go along with this. But after further discussion almost everybody went along with the demand, and after some more debate all went along. It looks as if it is determined now that we have to sign our names and join this association. But the way the situation is today, it might be the best thing to do. Wednesday we signed this declaration. *[As far as I can see from the data I have, whatever the prisoners signed at this point in time, was not binding and did not change anything in their protest against the Nazification of the schools. The efforts to make the teachers join the samband had now been dropped by the government and the Nazi had given up their plans about a new Storting. The battle was over. Was this episode just a face-saving device on the part of the local captors? It seems the teachers felt that signing this paper then would have no legal and moral consequences and did so to expedite the departure. For more detailed information about this, see Kirkenesferda pages 287 ff].*

It is being said now that we are going to return around the weekend, supposedly the 8th of August. But now the day has passed, and we're still here. So we have to be patient.

For a while we were quite optimistic, but now we are waiting again. As usual we are left with uncertainty, and it gets on our nerves. The end must be near now. We have sent a telegram to Eidsvoll, so now we think that we will get under way soon."

August 13.
"Many things have happened now since the last time I wrote. Risnes [A minister in the Quisling government] has given a speech here. [The teachers ignored him.]
Today money was handed out to the ones that will travel in the first group, and I.D. cards were returned. The weather is better, hope that will last. It is hard to believe we are now going to get away from here. Yesterday I was at a "party" in Goksøyr's tent. It was very pleasant. Fresh pollock, liver, coffee, bread and good butter, and in addition *molter!* [cloudberries]. Now I manage well. The food is very important under the circumstances in which we live here, and companionship and friendship are strengthened through sharing. A memory that will last for a long time." *[The food was smuggled in by the local residents]*

August 17.
"Monday again. Sunday we worked until 12. The weather looked terrible in the morning - there was a cloudburst during the night. After awhile it got lighter, so we didn't get soaked through and through. During the afternoon the weather improved. Otherwise the day passed like Sundays do. Sanden had a 30th wedding anniversary, and it so

happened that Fagerjord had got waffles, cookies and *molter* as a gift [from friends in Kirkenes], so we made coffee and had a good time. I gave a little speech for him, and he responded. But today a rather dark mood has been prevailing. Many had expected the travel to start today, but we are still kept in uncertainty. We had a good dinner, fresh pollack, that Jakobsen and I had bought. *[He does not explain how they "bought" it. Perhaps the guards were beginning to become more lax, letting the prisoners get by with more interaction with local people.]* The food was excellent. In addition, I bought a little bread - those things really help the spirits. I feel healthier and pretty strong. But I am bothered by the uncertainty and by homesickness. Otherwise no real complaints. When we think about how many other people in the world are suffering these days, then our problems become small. As usual a lot of rumors in the air. Fantastic rumors about *Hermann. [Camp "slang" for the Germans?]* Who knows what is true. There must be something to it. As for our return trip, the mill churns slowly, and it strains our patience."

August 23. [Last entry]

"Sunday. Fine weather, wind from the south and sunny. No mosquitoes and few flies. We had a good day. I got ill again Friday. I had salted *steinbit* [a fish] for dinner, and that I couldn't handle. I still have to be cautious with what I eat.

"More "certain" rumors: 143 of us are leaving at the beginning of next week. And that comes from the commandant, the doctor and his assistants. So now I almost

72

believe it. But it is better to take the attitude of a skeptic here, so the disappointment will not be too strong if it does not come about this time either. Otherwise life is going here as usual. From Ågot I got, which I think I've mentioned, a telegram-letter and that was a great pleasure. Everything is well at home, and that is a big consolation amidst all this uncertainty and waiting. Yesterday we had a birthday celebration in the tent. A.*[a fellow prisoner]* was 55. Coffee with canned milk and crackers. Sanden and I gave speeches for him. One feels strange and strong emotions up here, especially on Sundays and holidays – when one has time to collect one's thoughts. Small things can bring with them such strong associations that one has to pull oneself together not to cry. Especially memories from childhood days, home, and the ones that are dear to you, streaming forth so strongly that it takes strength not to become sentimental. In our present situation we are very receptive to that type of emotions.

I hope that this return trip will become a reality before the cold sets in here, and that all of us will get to leave at the same time, or about the same time."

This was the last entry in the diary. The first group to be returned left Kirkenes at the end of August. The rest of the teachers were sent home a couple of months later. They were transported back in ships under guard and experienced some air attacks from Russian planes on the way. My father's ship came close to being hit. According to one of the officers on board, one bomb just missed the ship due to a two second timing error. Most of the teachers were gradually reinstated in their schools, and they did not have to join the N.S. samband. The battle had been won. The attempts by the Germans and their Norwegian collaborators to Nazify Norway had suffered a severe set back.

About sources:

The first version of this document was published by the Western Viking, Seattle, Washington in June 2000, and I appreciate the permission to place it on the Net.

The events leading up to the arrest of the teachers, only briefly summarized here, are very dramatic. To readers of Norwegian who are interested in more details, I can recommend my main source:

Amundsen,S, Editor: *Kirkenesferda.* J.W. Cappelen Forlag Oslo 1946. The book is now out of print, but available in larger libraries.

For other relevant literature contact Deichmanske Bibliotek, Oslo. So far I have not been able to locate any books in English on the subject.

I am very grateful to my good friend Ivar Svare, professor at the University of Trondheim, for making available to me copies of notes made by his father, my father's colleague and fellow prisoner, about activities in the Eidsvoll area during the first days of the war, and along with that a copy of Helga Stenes' article "Den norske læreraksjonen for tyve år siden." (The arrest of Norwegian teachers twenty years ago), Aftenposten, Oslo, 2.19-20 1962,. and especially for locating a copy of *Kirkenesferda* in a second-hand bookstore in Norway and sending it all to me!

Cappelen Forlag has given me permission to use pictures from *Kirkenesferda* for this article.

Photo by Cynthia Brakstad

This plaque on a wall in Kirkenes says:

Erected by Norwegian teachers

In gratitude for all help the people of Sørvaranger gave to the 636 teachers in German captivity

28 Apr. - 4 Nov. 1942

TRYGVE HØGBERG:
A CLOAK-AND-LUGER PERSONA

by Anne Sophie Houdek, Inger-Lise Tendal, Rick Walker
and Astri Grieg Fry

At the height of the Nazi occupation of Norway in the early 1940s, German officers routinely commandeered desirable residences. Presidents Harbitz Gate 19, a fourth-story walkup apartment, was not overlooked.

During World War II, this became the residence of a prominent German officer. He was, as were many of his type, on the hit list of the Norwegian Resistance, headquartered in Sweden (as well as in Britain). These resistors planned and executed many disruptive sabotage operations during the occupation. One of their core members was Trygve Høgberg. He was given the assignment to travel to Oslo, pose as a telephone repairman and assassinate the German officer upon his return from the office expected in the early afternoon. Trygve, after presenting himself for the telephone repair, remained in the three-bedroom apartment into the early evening, several hours after his arrival. After raising suspicions for staying so long on the job, he finally gave up his vigil and left the building. Later on when meeting up with operatives over on Oslo's eastside, Trygve learned that the Germans were on to him, and had put the word out that he was to be apprehended, or more probably with his record, shot on sight.

Having thus been forewarned, he avoided the regular travel modes of autos, buses, and trains, donned a pair of skis and headed for Sweden. After a day, it came to his notice that several men appeared to be following him. As it turned dark early that time of year, Trygve skied on into the night, leaving his pursuers far behind.

He safely reached Kjesäter Castle in Sweden. Despite its neutrality, Sweden allowed Norwegian troops to train here, and Trygve assisted in admitting refugees to this transit center for the remainder of the war. A minority of these refugees were Norwegian Jews. Some of them became livelong friends of Trygve.

Thus Trygve had left behind the simple pleasures of hearth and home for a time—that is, if life in Norway during the war was simple in any way. For example, when celebrating New Year's Eve with family and friends in 1941, just before midnight the doorbell rang. Outside on the doorstep was only a flat package. It contained a gramophone record by which to listen to the king's annual Christmas speech to his beleaguered people. Originating in England, the record had been mailed via Stockholm and finally delivered by courier to the Høgberg home. Connections such as these to the outside world were vital to morale in occupied Norway.

It is small wonder that Trygve was a wanted man. Before his flight to Sweden, on more than one occasion he masqueraded in Nazi officer uniform, complete with Luger pistol, car and driver and entered Botsfengselet, one of Olso's prisons. Here he demanded loudly in German

77

—"Sofort, bitte!"—the instant release of some Resistance member, under the pretext of transfer to the Nazi headquarters at Viktoria Terrasse for interrogation. By producing falsified documents, he also was able to extract political inmates from other Oslo prisons: Møllergaten 19 and Akershus Fortress. At the latter location, however, the approach was in stark contrast to Botsfengselet maneuvers: scaling stone walls at night, moving by stealth, eluding guards in order to reach the incarcerated prisoners, many of whom were wanted by the Nazis for their intellectual influence.

After the liberation, the brilliant saboteur, Max Manus, mentioned Trygve by name in one of his books about the war, including revealing one of Trygve's wartime aliases: Gartner Kristensen. Moreover, Trygve was ceremoniously awarded several medals by King Haakon himself for his wartime service, at the Oslo Royal Palace.

So far this account has been related by Anne-Sophie Houdek and Inger-Lise Tendal, Trygve's daughters and his former son-in-law, Rick Walker. On the occasion of Trygve's 70th birthday, however, Norway's leading newspaper, *Aftenposten*, ran a full-page news article celebrating Trygve's life story. By then, Trygve was a prominent businessman, a buyer for a shoe retail outlet chain in Oslo and president and board member on several sports clubs. Trygve lost his first wife to illness in his fifties, but remarried and had his last child at the age of 59. He was a World Cup referee, could watch a game on television, listen to a game on the radio and read the paper for the previous day's results; all at the same time at age seventy. He had reserved tickets waiting for him at all soccer games in Oslo, and if invited, you had to be on guard for possible inadvertent kicking and head butting throughout the game.

On a side story, while pulling up 40 years of flooring in an old Victorian home in North Portland in the early 1980s, I, Rick, came across a news article under the first layer of linoleum. The paper had been rolled up to fill in depressions in the soft pine flooring before the new linoleum was laid down. In the rolled-up paper was an Oregonian article and pictures about the Germans parachuting into Fornebu Airport in Oslo as part of the invasion of Norway. On the opposite page was an article about the Norwegian Resistance, accompanied by a picture of several men standing in the snow by a tree. Trygve would have known them all.

On another curious side note, as told by Anne-Sophie: In the early 1950s my father returned to President Harbitz Gate 19, and at "this scene of an intended earlier crime," our family made its home in the very same apartment where my father Trygve had waited in vain for the Nazi occupant so many years earlier. Some family members came to reside in that apartment for decades.

THE VERY SPECIAL COURAGE OF
KNUT ROMANN-AAS

by Bjørn Bakke and Astri Grieg Fry

There must be many ways to display courage, but the most deserving may be the courage that remains behind the scenes. Such was the case of Knut Romann-Aas.

Although, after World War II, his wife was my English teacher, I knew him only peripherally as my parents' friend. He was a very young man when the war broke out in Norway in 1940. Prior to that he had studied in Germany, becoming fluent in German. This qualification became both his asset and liability.

When the Germans occupied our town of Raufoss (c. 55 miles north of Oslo), one of the main industries there was Raufoss Ammunisjonsfabrikker. Naturally the Germans wanted the continued production of ammunition and weapons for their military operations. To ensure this, they needed German-Norwegian interpreters, and Knut was set to work as such in the ammunition factory. Because he was regarded as being in German employ, at first he was resented by the workers there. What most people didn't know—Norwegians and Germans alike—was that he was a member of the Norwegian Underground Movement.

Knut's job description as interpreter included translating blueprints to Norwegian so that the Norwegians could work from them. However, beyond the technical descriptions, Knut also came across intelligence that proved most useful to the Norwegian Underground.

Therefore, Knut made it his business to steal away to an office with the blueprints, asking for three copies instead of the requisite two for the Germans. This third copy he would keep for himself and later smuggle out to Resistance members. The man who produced the copies at some point probably understood Knut's intention and somehow helped him keep his activities under wraps. This would have bought Knut some time, but eventually he was found out by the Germans. He actually was turned in by a fellow Norwegian, who also turned in about another twenty Norwegian Resistance fighters. By 1944 Knut was taken to the Akershus Fortress in Oslo, the equivalent of a death sentence from which there was no court of appeal.

While in Akershus, on a daily basis Knut would hear cell doors clanging open and shut as newly arrived prisoners were thrown into cells somewhere nearby. This alternated with the times when a cell door would open, one or more prisoners be removed, an action followed by the sound of gunshots. These occurrences took a tremendously emotional toll on Knut wondering when and if his turn might be next, and it is hardly surprising that after the war he suffered severely from post-traumatic stress disorder (PTSD). He endured this prison existence until the spring of 1945 when he and the other Akershus inmates were liberated.

After the war Knut was recognized by the people who knew what his real role during the war had been, but there remained those who continued to hold a grudge.

Despite his imprisonment, they refused to believe that he had not collaborated with the Nazis.

Years later, he did encounter his former German supervisor when the latter visited Norway. He had suspected what Knut's clandestine wartime activities had been, but without informing on him at the time. They became friends after that.

I regret that I did not learn the full story of Knut until after he died, when a book, *Krigens Redsler (The War's Horrors),* by Birger B. Rasmussen was written about him and four others engaged in similar activities. I like to think that, despite his PTSD, he was able to marry after the war and start a family. All the same, I wish I had known the truth about his heroism while he was still alive, if only to have shaken his hand and given him a pat on the back in recognition of his very special brand of courage.

Chapter 2: Rural Norway

ANNA MARIA SPILLING
by Pauline Coleman

Born Anna Eriksen, on 7 December, 1918 in Aurdal, Valdres, she was a young mother in 1942 when WW II was underway in Norway, the Germans having invaded the country in April 1940. Being of a proud people, and certainly not willing to give up without a fight, Anna chose to join the Norwegian Underground Movement, those people who dedicated their lives to resisting the Germans. (Anna's husband chose to join sides with the Nazis.)

Bjarne, her son, was just an infant and on this particular day it was Anna's responsibility to deliver papers advising others who also were working in the Underground what their next plan would be and when the next meeting would be held. Bjarne was in the buggy, and the papers she needed to deliver were under the mattress of the baby buggy. She had delivered some of the papers and was continuing on her walk with the baby to her next stop.

She came to a bakery and needed to be in touch with two men who worked there. Papers were tucked under her coat and she left the buggy right outside of the bakery and went in. The papers were carefully and slyly given to the men as they continued to make polite conversation.

One of the men happened to look out the window of the bakery and saw two German soldiers poking around the baby in the buggy. He alerted Anna at once and told her she must leave immediately by the back door of the bakery. Anna froze for a moment —and then said, "I cannot leave my baby . . . I must go!"

She walked out the front door and went to the buggy, and, with all the courage she could muster, took hold of the handle on the buggy. One of the German soldiers asked her if the baby was a boy or a girl. Anna replied it was a boy. The German soldier asked her how old he was. She told him. At this point Anna was sure something horrible was going to happen to both of them. She began to take a step pushing the buggy, and at that point he told her his wife in Germany had had their baby— but he had not yet seen it and it would be about the same age. As it turned out he just happened to be a soldier serving in the German Army who had a baby himself somewhere in Germany.

I'm sure Anna had many other stories to tell of hardships she endured during the German occupation . . . but this is the one that never leaves my mind when I think of her.

Anna arrived in the U.S.A. on the *SS Stavangerfjord* on July 10, 1950. She became a naturalized citizen on January 24, 1956. Anna became a close friend to all of us in our Norwegian community and here at Norse Hall. Anna married Thomas Spilling, a member of Grieg Lodge, on May 29, 1958. Tom died in 1991 and Anna died this past January 2, 2015, at the age of 97.

VALDRES, NORWAY, DURING WORLD WAR II
by Kirsti Kumar and Astri Grieg Fry

At the onset of WW II, I was six and the oldest of several siblings. We, the Lien family, lived on a small dairy farm in Valdres, Norway. We had butter, cheese and livestock in the form of goats and pigs. Unlike the rationing in the cities, we did not experience a food shortage. During the first summer of the war, two boys about twelve and fourteen were sent to us from Oslo. They were under-nourished, with pink circles around their eyes. We were curious about these boys because they were so thin, but with good food they started looking better. As a result, my parents were pleased. By summer's end the boys returned to Oslo. Some other children stayed with other families; they were younger and they stayed longer. (There was a charitable organization behind these visits, but I'm not sure which.)

My family was religious and my grandfather read to us from the Bible every Sunday. We could only attend church about once a month as the local pastor rotated between several churches. When we did attend a church service, the visiting boys squirmed and giggled. I don't think they quite knew what to make of the services.

Before the war, we had a radio, but now we were not allowed to own one. My parents and grandfather and two aunts packed our radio inside clothing and attic insulation and placed it within a wooden crate. The radio was hidden in the woods next to a nearby field. Here stones had been deposited from clearing the land, *stein teigen*. I was not supposed to know about this concealment, but I did know and never told anyone. When the war was over, this was the first thing to be checked, and it worked. It was so exciting when it was taken out! It was plugged in and worked right away.

The war was a difficult time regarding clothing and shoes. There was just one time when we got a package from the US, possibly through the Red Cross. We had relatives in South Dakota: my grandfather's brother and his wife and their families. We all got something, and I got a pink blouse. Included in the package was a little sugar, coffee and powdered cocoa. No ski boots were to be had. We had to use reindeer hide for ski boots and improvised ski bindings. It was sad for me that I could ski very little. That was almost the only form or recreation we had during the long winters—both slalom and cross country, and junior ski jumping. We did our best with our limited equipment and whatever time was allowed.

There was no money; it was taken. Once I wanted to go a summer camp. This cost five kroner which we didn't have, but somehow I still got to go. My friend was the teacher's daughter and I went with her. We took a bus, about 50 km away to the camp, and stayed for one week.

We had no car, only horses. People owning cars were not allowed to use them. My teacher had a car in his garage. There it sat during the war. We were not allowed to have a Syttende Mai parade until the war was over, and we could celebrate again.

We delivered our milk in pails with lids to the nearby dairy, which then made the butter and cheese. At one point, the Germans came and wanted to bomb this dairy. A bomb was dropped, but went into the lake, Vangsmjøsa. From the pressure of the bomb's impact, the windows were blown out of the dairy, and the noise and vibration affected the whole community. I never did find out what the Germans' motive for this bombing was.

We were not allowed to keep our crops, especially potatoes. Once a German came to inspect our farm along with a Norwegian interpreter, and we children were scared by the idea of Norwegians who were friendly with the Germans. My dad was out plowing in the field, and so my three-year-old brother was told by these visitors to fetch him. "Do it yourself!" retorted this simple son of the soil, not knowing that he was expected to obey their commands. The German was too heavy to go there, however, and so they left.

Other visitors we had were Gypsies, and we children were afraid we might get lice from them! My father fed their horses, gave them food, and they used our kitchen to prepare their food. They stayed only one night, and such visits might happen once a year during the war.

Often there were planes overhead, at any time during the day. We children were always counting them; sometimes there were as many as twenty-four. We used blackout curtains, except during the shortest nights in the summer time. One summer night we three sisters and my brother were in bed, but our mother was still up. A plane flew so low that night that it looked like it would come through the window. My mother threw herself on top of us children convinced that the end had come, but the plane flew on without hitting the house.

Throughout the war, young Norwegian men of twenty or older were sent to Germany. Some did not return, and a distant cousin was one of these—assigned to the German Frontline. Others who had to go did return.

A TELEMARK FAMILY: *Torleiv Veum is my first cousin, born in Fyresdal, Telemark, on 3 January, 1935. His father was my mother's oldest brother. Fyresdal was also the traitor Vidkun Quisling's hometown. Torleiv's account "Minna fra krigstida," Wartime Memories, was written at least ten years ago.*

Knut Austad, 2015

WARTIME MEMORIES
by Torleiv Veum; translated by Astri Grieg Fry

I was five at the onset of the war, 9 April, 1945. Pappa came from the telephone and related that war had broken out. I had seen airplanes, several numbers of them from before, and had heard about bombing. It was only much later that we could gain a better understanding of cause and effect. At that time, our attention was more focused on our daily lives: our childhoods, clothing, shoes, food and school attendance.

There were many problems between the school authorities and teachers during the war. The teachers needed to belong to the correct political party. Education suffered under the Nazi occupation, a number of teachers were discharged; whereas others, approved by the Nazis, were hired in their place. In our local school there was a bookcase, containing the school library, with a couple of shelves with Nazi books. From these shelves, no one touched a single book, nor were any of them ever borrowed to be read at home.

When our pastor was deposed by the Nazis, all church activity ceased: christenings, confirmations, and church services in general. The Nazis installed a pastor of their own, but only Nazi sympathizers attended his services. On the occasions of baptisms and funeral processions, laics performed the offices of the church. Now, with the Nazi pastor Flatland installed, the parsonage was surrounded by a chickenwire fence and barbed wire, just as at Lunden, Quisling's home, and two vicious dogs were tethered in front of the house. Another Nazi also lived there, a hated and feared man. The Germans ordered that all weapons and radios were to be turned over to the sheriff, and we did not see these items again until 1945.

In addition to our Gimle School, the Germans requisitioned all the houses nearby. These were to be used as a concentration camp for Russian prisoners of war. The barbed wire enclosure around the school was huge, 3-4 meters high, and of a special type which was impossible to scale. There were about 30 German soldiers and guards, and roughly 100 prisoners in deplorable burlap clothing and shoes. The prisoners were driven to the woods to fell lumber, whereas the forest owners were ordered by the Germans to provide this supply of trees. The prisoners were overseen by armed German guards.

The Russian prisoners were artistic and creative: they made rings of aluminum tobacco boxes and some wonderful birds whittled from wood. These items were used as barter with people who smuggled food to them. We kids had the chance to give the Russians food: some of our school lunch, or some bread from home. Amongst us, we counted up who had the most rings, tobacco boxes and the most beautiful birds. Once when I was there trading bread for a prospective tobacco box, I put my bread loaf down. Suddenly a prisoner jumped from the truck, seized my loaf and stuffed it inside of his pants. He jumped back on the truck, whereupon a German soldier beat him with his rifle. I suspect the Germans ate good Norwegian farm bread that evening. At the end of the day, the Russians would march back to camp about the time school was over.

We got to know the German guards, and knew those who were "kind" and allowed us to pass food to the prisoners, versus those who were strict and scared us away. Occasionally we got a ride next to the driver of a prisoner transport truck. But another time, when the prisoners were accompanied by one of the "kind" guards, he suddenly raised his rifle to his shoulder and trained it on us. Our reaction was immediate. We threw ourselves into the nearest snow drift and then fled further on into the woods.

During the war there was an absence of imported goods, and rationing of what still was for sale: sugar, tobacco, coffee, clothing and shoes, and substitutes for many things—coffee, flour and sugar. This lack of sugar caused us youngsters to become absolutely wild for something sweet. If you ever could find something sweet, it was wonderful. At home I came across a little sugar that had been stored in a chest and I licked the entire inside of it, but it was difficult to extract the traces from the corners. Mamma did what she could to provide sweets for us kids at

Christmas. She saved the rationed sugar and made wonderful Holiday caramels, hanging them in decorative baskets on the tree.

One time German soldiers came to our farm to buy food: apples and turnips. Pappa wouldn't sell them anything, he explained that he had already made his enforced delivery and couldn't sell any more food. I believe the Germans accepted this explanation.

Tobacco was in short supply, and I remember the men drying rhubarb leaves in the stove oven to make tobacco from. My dad used nicotine sulphate for spraying the fruit trees and this was used as a nicotine additive to the rhubarb tobacco. Beer was also brewed during the war.

The Germans made us account for both our livestock as well as harvest. They handed out paper sacks to be filled with apples for them. Farmers filled them with earth and rocks, and placed apples on the top. The "German apples" were stored in our school for a time, which we attended every other day. Eventually there were holes in the bags, and apples, earth and rocks went all over the floor. We kids had to fill new bags, and we were told to leave out the dirt. However, the adult supervising looked the other way and said nothing after we had filled them up with the layers as before.

We kids played all over our farm. The barn was a popular playground. We created tunnels in the hay and had many clever hiding places. Once, however, there were sheep tied up there, in one of my best hiding places. I couldn't understand this, and asked Pappa about it. He told me to hold my tongue; the sheep were hidden away because the Germans were coming to count livestock. I got the strictest order that it was utterly dangerous to say anything at all.

Because of our farm, we had better food than kids in town who would try to take it from us at school.

On the cars were mounted gas generators, heated by burning wood. On buses and trucks these generators were larger tanks, mounted on the back or the side of the vehicle. The gas from the generator passed through pipes to the cylinders of the cars. This procedure had to be started well before one wanted to start the car.

The adults often spoke of Vidkun Quisling, especially in summertime, when he stayed at Lunden. I well remember riding on the bus and seeing the chickenwire fence with the barbed wire at the top which had been erected along the road leading to Lunden. His bodyguards in black uniforms stood watch along the Lunden driveway. Quisling's guards' vehicles weren't powered by generators such as we had to make do with. They had real gas, just like the Germans did. I once saw a cortege of three cars, with Quisling himself seated between two guards in the middle car.

Apparently during the spring of 1944, Quisling's guards arrested Pappa and Grandpa. The men in their black uniforms came and took them both down to Jonsborg. They returned that night, after having been interrogated personally by Vidkun Quisling. Pappa was accused of having worn a flower in his lapel on King Haakon's birthday, plus having fraternized with our deposed pastor. After the interrogation, Quisling had said, "Send them to Skien," but they were released anyway. Finally he had said, "I won't be too hard on the local people."

Later in the fall of 1944, Pappa and two of my uncles were ordered to come to the school. No one knew why, and everyone expected them home that evening. Mamma later related that one uncle had problems with his nerves after this arrest. He had been implicated in receiving parachute drops of supplies from England just before and was afraid the Germans knew about this. Several of our local inhabitants who were arrested after this raid knew about weapon and supply drops; but no one talked, as far as I know. That time my mother cried, which made an indelible impression on me. I don't believe I had ever seen her cry before, and seldom since. Mamma related that she had heard of Norwegian civilians being tortured.

Pappa did not expect to return home that evening. He asked permission to change his clothing before going down to the school, and gave instructions for hiding our illegal radio which was listened to in order to hear the news from England. The radio was hidden in a haystack. Many others were arrested in our area. When Pappa later was released, that was a happy day; but Uncle Halfdan was imprisoned for a month, and Uncle Tjostolv was sent to the Oslo prison camp, Grini.

Eventually our family found how we could help send packages to Uncle Tjostolv in Grini: one package of tobacco and one laundry detergent package, respectively, was allowed. Tricks were employed in order to provide prisoners with food, for example, the detergent package was steamed open and food placed there instead.

Throughout the war, the adults did and said much which didn't bear repeating, about more or less illegal activities. I constantly was told: "You mustn't say anything, anywhere." The fear of the Nazis was always with us. In the spring of 1945, however, many rumors circulated, and we kids understood that the war was taking a different course. The adults were no longer as guarded in their speech in our presence. Once our uncle Jon gave us a little chocolate which could not be bought anywhere. I naturally asked where he had got it. "From England," he said, "but you mustn't tell anyone." We didn't, as we had become deathly afraid of talking about anything illegal.

One day we heard that Hitler was dead. Now we could expect either peace or an invasion. Many believed that England would invade Norway. Uncle Tjostolv returned from Grini, some days before the peace was declared. He was frighteningly thin. Although he was a small man, I think he weighed under 50 kilos. I also remember that he had bite marks from cockroaches or lice. The Germans had by now surrendered in Denmark, and we all wondered what would happen here in Norway. Mamma began brewing beer. We needed some for the impending jubilation celebration. The morning of 7 May I got the shock of my life. In our living room was a radio, placed on the middle of the table. I rushed toward it as I knew this was perilous if the Nazis should find out. But later in the afternoon, we heard the news: "THERE IS PEACE!" What a relief, and I yelled, "I found the radio!" Our flag, which had been hidden somewhere, was hoisted. It had been banned for five years. We kids couldn't even remember having seen it before. It was in the middle of the spring planting, this fantastic day; but the men, plowing with the animals in the fields, unharnessed the horses, and took a holiday immediately. Mamma told me to run to some neighbors to invite them to dinner to celebrate the liberation. I ran right over, but avoided houses where I knew there were Nazis. I didn't waste any time on this errand!

Even though the official day of peace was 8 May, it was this evening of 7 May that I remember. We sang "Ja, vi elsker," and our "National Hymn of Norway," and "Norway in red, white, and blue." Uncle Tjostolv started wearing an armband with the Norwegian flag on it, and was armed. He was a member of the Home Front. He had new English boots, and a brown parachute. This was used to make shirts from. But the best part was crackers and chocolate from tins. We now often saw people in English uniforms. They came down from the hills and had that military bearing. In that spring of peace, the English and Norwegian soldiers took over Quisling's home, Lunden.

Tjostolv, even though he had been weakened by his imprisonment in Grini, was much occupied with the Home Front. The German soldiers surrendered their weapons, and the gates of the concentration camp were opened. People collected clothing for the Russian prisoners. The Home

96

Front arrested the Nazis, and put them to work transporting English weapons and equipment down from the hills. The arrest of the caretaker at the parsonage, Meidell, was dramatic. He came out on the stairs with a pistol in his hand. Our soldiers fired several times, and I think Meidell was hit before he gave himself up.

Before Syttende Mai that year, there was considerable sewing going on for us kids, from the parachute silk or whatever other material was at hand. We also got care packages from America.

Syttende Mai, 1945 was a tremendous day. Everyone was in downtown Fyresdal that day, many in uniform, and the Home Front soldiers with their flag armbands on. For us kids, the highlight was the handing out of English chocolate at the parsonage. There was also a ceremony next to some new graves in the churchyard. Russian prisoners at Gimle had died and had been buried in the woods. Their remains were moved to the churchyard, and there was a military ceremony there that day.

Another celebration of the peace for us was to travel to Skien for a collective family picture, in June 1945.

MEMORIES FROM WORLD WAR II
by Knut Austad

Norway's involvement in World War II has mostly been referred to as the German occupation. While that is basically true, the Germans did have a considerable number of native-born Norwegian helpers. However, although government at both the state and local levels was run to a certain extent by the Norwegian Nasjonal Samling (NS), Hitler and his Reichskommissar, Josef Terboven, still exercised ultimate control.

The NS was a legitimate political party established in 1933 by Vidkun Quisling. Its main focus was on Norwegian greatness and ethnic superiority. Its symbol was the Sun Cross, a yellow cross on a red background. The party was also a "strongman" party, proclaiming obedience to its Leader and disdain for democracy. The party was strongly anti-communist, or anti-Bolshevik. From about 1935 on, the NS adopted more and more of the German Nazi ideology, such as fear and hatred of Jews.

During the war, Quisling, with his NS party, was Head of State some of the time (naturally not recognized by the exiled Norwegian government in London). Quisling also had his "Hird," a black-clad paramilitary organization, established by the NS.

Quisling and his NS were in many ways a thorn in the side of the Germans. There were ongoing political conflicts between the two factions throughout the war. Quisling and Terboven had to work together because Hitler personally said so. Reichskommissar Terboven reported directly to Hitler.

Vidkun Quisling and Reichskommissar Terboven inspecting a division of the Norwegian paramilitary group known as the "Hird."   Photo: National Archives of Norway

In the following I have used Nazi as a generic name for the occupiers, the German military, and the Gestapo, unless I definitely knew who was doing what.

    The Nazis clearly wanted to control the local government by replacing everybody with their members. While replacement of the civil service including the police, teachers and clergy was largely unsuccessful, the Nazis oversaw every detail of what the local government was doing. Any violation of the Nazi rules was subject to dismissal and arrest, which often resulted in torture and death of the person, within Norway and in concentration camps in Germany.

I, Knut Austad, grew up in Valle, Setesdal, a place that for many years was isolated in a narrow valley, and as such retained a very old fashioned dialect. Its local culture was very chauvinistic. Not for nothing did Valle have the highest percentage of NS members in all of Norway including many community leaders. I believe this was primarily due to the focus on Norwegian greatness and ethnic superiority.

My very first memory of World War II was going with some adults to the store, and they talked about a war having broken out. There was talk about "Russfelt" (Roosevelt), and Stalin and Hitler. It was September 1, 1939. I did not understand anything beyond that, after all I was only a month short of five.

The next event was April 9, 1940 when the Germans invaded Norway. My parents were away at the mountain cabin, and we kids were home with a babysitter. Somebody got the word to Mom and Dad. Dad had a car, and was asked to, or volunteered to, drive to Kristiansand to fetch up refugees. Dad made more than one trip. The refugees were women and children. Some stayed with us at our house. I mostly remember teenage girls from Flekkeröya, a suburb of Kristiansand, near a military outpost. Kristiansand is 100 miles to the south; roads were very narrow and bad. Kristiansand was being bombed, but nobody knew how extensive the bombing was going to be. The bombing of Kristiansand did not last long. The refugees left, probably by bus.

My dad was a vicar in the Norwegian Church. He had also received officer's training before he went to the seminary. When war broke out, Dad reported for military duty, but the Norwegian military told him he was more needed as a pastor right were he was. A neighbor had to report for military duty. I remember his mother was crying. After a few days, maybe weeks, the neighbor returned home without having experienced any war activity.

There was no military action in our community, not close enough that we could see it. We did hear that the Bykle bridge was blown up by the Norwegian army. This completely severed the road from upper Setesdal to Telemark. Vinje in Telemark saw some military action. Pretty soon the "war" was over; no more Norwegian soldiers. German soldiers came.

A few weeks after the war had started, the occupation forces decided that they needed housing for about thirty German soldiers. And since a vicarage was considered state property, they requisitioned two bedrooms in the vicarage to house the soldiers. The vicarage was large, there were altogether five bedrooms, and the soldiers had their own sleeping bags or air mattresses. Nevertheless, refusing was not an option. Based upon what happened to other vicars, our family would just have been evicted had we refused, wearing only the clothes we had on at the time. Imprisonment at that time would not have been likely.

It must have been frightening for parents living in a house full of foreign soldiers, who had weapons and power. Mom and Dad only knew a few words of German, and the

German soldiers knew no Norwegian. But the soldiers behaved correctly. There was no carousing, no drinking, no assault. They had machine guns set up in our front yard, but that appeared to be for maintenance only, not as a line of defense. By that time the "hot war" activity had subsided, at least in Southern Norway.

The soldiers had chocolate, and they were not reluctant to share, which was very popular with us kids: myself at five, and my younger brothers, three and one. The soldiers helped by teaching my youngest brother to walk, even though this did not leave any tendency to march on his part. The soldiers took their trucks to the river for washing; we got to ride with them in the back of the military trucks. Great fun! One of the young soldiers spent a lot of time in our kitchen wildly flirting with my mom and our maid. They were very charmed by him. They got to know his name: "Kunkel Willy," Mom said. Probably his name was really was Willy Kunkel. The soldiers had their own military provisions including a large stack of the Swedish Wasa crackers. I still eat those, never forgetting where I first tasted them.

The legitimate Valle *lensmann*, or sheriff, was not held in high esteem, he was considered rather dumb. His wife was considered plain stupid. The local humor was merciless towards the sheriff and his wife. They had two sons who were in their teens when the war started. The sheriff was not a member of the NS. The NS did not make special efforts to remove non-NS members; they wanted cooperation, and they wanted the country to function as normal. But on their terms. The local non-NS sheriff stayed on. One time two Russian POWs had escaped into the mountains, and the sheriff was ordered to arrest them. And the sheriff did so. He went after them, found them and handed them over to the Nazis. The local non-NS in the community were outraged. They said, and rightfully so, the sheriff might have to go after the POWs, but he did not have to find them. Another incident was when the sheriff was ordered to arrest the non-NS teachers, including his next-door neighbor. He did. People said he could easily have got his son to whisper word to the neighbor to go hiking for a couple of days. But no, he just followed orders. The non-NS community put pressure on him to resign, which he then did.

Another local NS member was appointed sheriff. He had an interesting background. His direct line ancestor, living on the same farm, bearing the same name, was Olav K. Tveiten (1758-1837)—not only the local sheriff back then, but also a representative at the Eidsvold Council of 1814. So the new sheriff was of an old sheriff's family. He lived in the outskirts of town where the Germans built a watchtower on his property. It was well known that German uniformed personnel were staying with him there during the later part of the war. The good Norwegians suspected though that he got a lot of liquor from the Germans. But all the while, the new sheriff kept things calm. People felt relatively safe as long as they did not break the Nazi laws. I can never remember being afraid of the sheriff, nor did we ever see him accompanied by the German soldiers. We just knew they were there. We would sometimes see German military personnel on the road, but we never felt directly threatened by them. But you had to be very careful with what you said, and to whom you said it. There were people, party members and non-party members, who would report to the sheriff about who said what to whom.

We had to cover the windows with thick black paper even in our town deeply hidden between tall mountains. We did not have electricity, just kerosene lamps and candles. We still had to keep the windows covered at all times. One time we got a big laugh; one man reported his neighbor for uncovered windows, but it turned out it was just moonlight being reflected. A *stev*, a rhyme of four lines, was made and sung in our local dialect:

> *Dei på Haugland hev' glöymt å blende,*
> *da' måge sekk attför månen hengje.*
> *Og enkjemannen va' nummer ein,*
> *han melde grannen for månen skein.*

> The Haugland folk forgot to cover up windows,
> they should have hung a blanket over the moon.
> The widower was one of a kind,
> reporting his neighbor when the moon was shining.

When the war was over, the sheriff was arrested. But since he had not committed any crimes beyond being an NS member, he was released shortly after. The "old" sheriff got his job back, but only reluctantly. People remembered him following Nazi orders too well during the war.

It took a long time before consumer goods were available. I needed some part for my bicycle, one I had put together from parts. I heard that the ex-sheriff might have what I needed, I went to visit him and actually we became good friends. It was at his house I first started listening to and liking Norwegian folk music, the Hardanger fiddle type.

Regular radio receivers were only allowed by NS members. In Norway all radios were registered; there was an annual fee to be paid for having a radio. (TV only started about 1958.) Consequently, authorities knew exactly who owned a radio, and it was therefore easy to collect all radios from those who were not members of the NS. The word came: "Deliver your radio at a central location." Apparently the radios were stored locally; as soon as the war was over, we got our little Tandberg radio back in good shape. King Haakon of Norway was broadcasting freedom speeches from London during the war, with the BBC reporting "truths." The NS and the Germans feared that. Some people had radios hidden away, listening and spreading words about what they heard. This was highly illegal and subject to arrest.

My paternal grandparents lived 25 miles away. We kids, with or without our parents, traveled by bus to those grandparents. Such travel was unrestricted and safe. That travel, even though it was only 25 miles, took about one hour. Mom's parents, however, lived more than 100 miles away, and in another county, so neither my mom nor we kids got to visit those grandparents until the war was over. Travel permissions were granted during the war, but only if you had a very legitimate reason.

One night in 1943, an unknown man came riding from the forest up to our house. Without introducing himself or dismounting from his horse, he just said. "Please tell Mrs. Austad that three of her brothers were arrested last night. One, I think his name was Jon, escaped." Then he rode off. Later on, probably by letter, did we hear that Jon had received word and had gone into hiding. Two of the uncles were released after a few weeks, but the third was sent to Grini, the main NS concentration camp near Oslo. He spent over two years there and was not released until the war was over.

Uncle Jon had a mountain cabin that was broken into by what looked like a hand grenade thrown at the door lock. The door was never replaced; however, it was repaired by a really good carpenter. After the war, Uncle Jon kept the door in place. He never repainted it, the scars from the German hand grenade showing clear memories of the war. By the way, nobody was there at the cabin when it was broken into, nor do I know if anything "illegal" was found. But there was a fair amount of "illegal" activity going on in that area. This was Vidkun Quisling's home village, the same place my mother came from, and Quisling had a residence there. At least one time Quisling "invited" my grandpa and my uncle for a talk at his residence. He wanted to persuade my grandfather to join

106

and support the Nazis. "Don't you know I can have you arrested?" Quisling threatened. "I am 75 years old and I have my God, and there is nothing you can do to scare me," Grandpa answered. Documents found after the war said that the Nazis considered Grandpa and his sons "dangerously uncooperative."

When the war ended, Quisling's residence was undergoing extensive remodeling. With my uncle who was just released from Grini, I got a chance to go in there and look around. Mostly I remember the chain link fence around it with barbed wire on top and in the living room, an enormous fireplace built of marble. It would have been a gorgeous residence had it been completed. The building is still there; since the war it has been owned by Abraham Quisling, Vidkun's nephew, who was not a member of the Nazis.

Statspolitiet, the State Police, was established in 1932 as a national police force primarily to quell labor conflicts. In 1941 Statspolitiet became entirely controlled by the Nazis. Statspolitiet became an armed police force modeled after the German Gestapo. Its main focus was political adversaries, prison escapees, espionage, sabotage or anything else considered resistance to the NS and the German occupation. Statspolitiet functioned as a separate police force, administrated separately from the local police and Quisling's Hird.

The local police force had both NS members and non-NS members on the force, though it was ultimately controlled by NS. The Germans had their own Gestapo which was under control by Reichskommissar Terboven.

My father, as a vicar in the Norwegian Church like most clergymen there, took a stand against the German occupation by reading in church the manifestos issued by Kristent Samråd, the Christian Council. This consisted basically of reading from the church pulpit anti-NS proclamations issued by the Church Council. This resulted in nine interrogations by Odd Ferdinand Brandsborg (in his twenties) and his Statspoliti colleagues from Kristiansand. Mr. Brandsborg established an office at the hotel and "requested" my father's presence there. One time, I believe that was the last one and towards the end of the war, my father was told he was going to be arrested and taken to the regional headquarters in Kristiansand. He was told to go home and get ready. "Then we'll come by and pick you up," Brandsborg said. Any idea of escaping at that point was unthinkable, my mother would surely be arrested and we kids sent off somewhere.

I remember my father getting dressed, with overcoat, hat and a small suitcase, pacing back and forth in the back yard waiting to be picked up by Statspolitiet. Mom was crying, the one and only time I can remember my mother crying. But Brandsborg never showed up. After a couple of hours my father called the hotel and asked why. He was then told they had changed their mind for now, but they would come and get him later. My brother, though younger than me, but with a lot more knowledge of WW II history, says that the local NS sheriff interfered at the time,

108

and convinced Brandsborg not to arrest my father. Whatever the reason, my father never was arrested. He was harassed and threatened, but not arrested or physically tortured. After the war, Brandsborg was sentenced to 12 years of forced labor, but like most, both Germans and Norwegians, served much less time.

Three young men from Valle went to the Eastern Front to fight with the Germans. One of them was killed. The other two I knew quite well. One of them, Torjus, was known as a wild young teen before the war. He didn't do anything really bad, he was just an incorrigible hellion. Torjus joined the NS as a 16-year-old, just as the war started. One time he was home on leave, wearing a German uniform, being drunk and weaving his handgun around and shooting at rats. In spite of this, I never heard anybody being scared of him. Not even when he said he was going over to the Bedehus, Church Annex, to shoot the pastor. The pastor was my dad. I never heard that he actually did go over to the Bedehus, people mostly laughed about it, everybody knew Torjus—he's one of us, so there would be no problem. In February 1946 the local newspaper announced that Torjus had been sentenced to 2 ½ years in prison. A young girl neighbor of his, and being from a non-NS family, said that she thought the prison sentence was awfully long. She did express the general sentiment in the village. The war is over, let's all forget about it. And after all, Torjus was one of us. After the war, Torjus served time in a prison camp where he was trained as a carpenter. Afterward the war he married a well-to-do widow and made a career as a home builder. The last time I saw him, I was a teenager and hitched a ride with him from Kristiansand to Valle. We had a great time. He sure was "a jolly good fellow," all things considered.

The third front soldier got sick on the Eastern Front. After the war he had one lung and one kidney removed, and maybe some other things. Doctors gave him at most five years to live. He never worked again, he also told my mother that he would gladly have served his time in jail if he could have kept his health. But, lo and behold, the last time I heard about him, it must have been in the 1980s, he was still alive.

Our family had a car during the war, but it never was "our car." It was Dad's. Mom never learned to drive, and never wanted to. The car was the only thing in our family over which Dad had absolute authority. An eager car salesman from Kristiansand talked my father into trading his almost new little Ford Junior, model 1937, for a one-year-old 1938 Chevrolet. This was in 1939. So for that time and place, my dad's car was indeed something special.

One night, my father came home and wanted my mother to see the damage to the car. He had been in a collision. The lower part of the front fender was all banged up. This was before the war started in Norway. Dad told how it happened: An oncoming car came at high speed, and was unable to stop in time. Mind you, the roads at that time were so narrow that passing was only possible using extreme caution. The other driver spoke with an accent. He seemed very nervous, apologized profusely, and insisted on

110

paying for the damage in cash and on the spot. No police necessary. In retrospect it is not hard to figure this out. A German intelligence agent, AKA spy, on the job. Someone who did not wish the authorities to poke into his business.

When the invasion started on April 9,1940, word went out for volunteers to transport refugees from Kristiansand to Valle. Kristiansand was being bombed. Then as the "hot war" stopped, the Germans kept track of the cars in Norway. My dad's car was new and very valuable. The German military placed a large yellow sticker over the windshield, stating that this car was confiscated by the German military and must not be moved, unless ordered by a German Officer of a certain rank. The car stayed in the garage and the war went on. One day in the summer, probably 1944, our front yard was full of German soldiers. They had finally gotten the authority to pick up the car. They pushed it out of the garage, but could not get it started. Some essential parts were missing, such as the battery and the starter. Upon demand, my dad told them that the local sheriff had requested the missing parts, and Dad had gotten a receipt for them. So the soldiers left. Who pushed the car back into the garage, I don't remember, but it was put back there. The German soldiers went to see the sheriff. The German military had somewhat of a permanent station on the sheriff's property. Apparently, the sheriff convinced them that he needed these parts. Not only that, the sheriff maintained the he needed that car for a new patrol car. Somehow he managed to get the Germans' OK to apply for such a transfer. But the NS bureaucracy was not any more efficient than other government bureaucracies, so the application lingered. Finally, in early 1945 it seemed that the sheriff had received permission from the NS authorities to pick up the car. The sheriff's son was talking big about getting the car, but by then it seemed that the sheriff was no longer in a hurry. The war ended and the car was still in the garage. After the war, the sheriff said that he never intended to get the car, he did it just to save the car for my dad. Dad called this BS. The truth, like so often, was probably somewhere in between. As the war was ending, the sheriff most likely decided that now was not a good time to exercise more power grabs.

Against all odds, Dad's car then stayed safely in the garage throughout the war. (Actually it was in good shape till I wrecked it in 1953.)

Regarding our education during the war, our teacher was a man and a member of NS. He got the position because of "the party book." Otherwise he was a licensed teacher. We children did not notice much about the teacher being NS. I remember seeing NS propaganda literature being sent to the school, but I do not remember that any of these books were used in class. Nor do I remember the teacher talking about NS nor the war in school. Fourth grade was the last of the war for me.

In my "little school" we were about 15 students. Two came from NS homes, one girl and one boy. The girl's father was known as an avid NS member. His daughter was very quiet and said almost nothing. She seemed lonely and depressed. The boy's family were more "membership only." The boy was bullied sometimes, but mostly for telling "tales," but with no political overtones.

The teacher was not the best teacher I have ever had, but he was far from the worst. When the war ended, he lost his teacher's license. Most teachers got their licenses back after a relatively short time, but our teacher seemed to give up. He never married, never moved away from Valle, and died fairly young. I think of him with sadness.

The vicars in the Norwegian Church were salaried civil servants. In addition to their Church duties, vicars also had a number of public duties, such as keeping official registry of births, weddings and deaths. In country communities, vicars also served as what is now known as Children's Services Division. Most vicars in the Norwegian Church resigned from their salaried positions as protest against NS. It may seem strange that most of them stayed in their vicarages and were allowed to conduct their clerical duties. The reason for that was, like it was in many cases with teachers, NS did not have enough members to fill in. So even though I as a small child did not understand it, the family income disappeared with my father's resignation. The formal resignation consisted of refusing to accept a salary from the NS-controlled government.

The vicarage had a small farm that created a living for a family of three: the tenant farmer Margit, an elderly widow and her two grown sons. Margit decided from the goodness of her heart to split the vicarage farm with us, so that our family could produce food to eat. My parents then became farmers. We had up to three cows, always one pig, and chickens. My parents had both grown up on farms, and were well acquainted with farm work. This way we were never hungry during the war. That being said, the only food available was what could be produced then and there. That included some berry picking and a little fishing. The climate being cold, we could grow barley, oat, potatoes, carrots, cabbage and rhubarb. Tomatoes, wheat and all kinds of "normal fruits and vegetables" would not grow in Valle.

Everything was rationed. During the first of the war years we could get some stuff, but pretty soon the stores were empty. For children, the absence of sugar and chocolate was the worst; for the grownups, missing tobacco and coffee was the worst. Food-wise, that is. We learned a new German word for substitution: "*Ersatz.*" Mostly in connection with coffee that the grownups complained bitterly about. Leather for shoes was almost nonexistent. Shoes often had soles made of wood and the rest from paper. Such shoes did not work well in winter and rainy days.

The concept of *matauk*, food increase, was necessary all over Norway. It was also strongly encouraged and supported by the NS government. Some of the new ways were interesting. We found out that the magpie bird was able to count her number of eggs, and their color. But she could not discriminate size. So kids and young adults would take two chicken eggs, color them green and black, and remove two of the magpie eggs for the chicken eggs. Two eggs was what someone had figured out that the

114

magpie could handle. Then we waited 21 days, and with a little bit of luck, two chicks were found in the magpie nest.

Tobacco was hard to come by. Some people would dry rhubarb leaves and smoke it in lieu of tobacco. Towards the end of the war tobacco seedlings became available. Both kids and adults would grow tobacco during the summer. A corporation was formed, Norsk-Engelsk Tobakksfabrikk, Neto. This company would accept Norwegian-grown tobacco. Payment would be in cash. Adult smokers were able to ship their homegrown tobacco to Neto and receive some readymade tobacco as part of the payment. In early May, 1945 Neto placed an ad in the paper announcing that they would no longer accept Norwegian-grown tobacco.

Raising rabbits was another new industry. Rabbit meat was OK to eat, but it did not taste that good. Rabbit skin was cured and made into clothes. Mostly girl's clothes, such as hats and jackets and coats. These were warm and often cute, I thought. We did not have many German soldiers in Valle. After the war I heard that many German soldiers in Norway were also short of food, and tried to buy rabbit food from the local kids. But the kids did not much like the German soldiers, so they would kill cats and sell cat meat to the German soldiers. But the Germans were not that gullible, and were quoted as saying *"Nix mehr pus!"* "No more pussycat!"

Mothers would cut up worn clothes, such as coats, suits, skirts and dresses, and sew "new" ones for the smaller children. Even as late as my high school days I remember this being done. One neat thing mothers did with dresses and skirts. Cut off the bottom 5" all around, inserting a 3-4" border of a bright different color. The daughter had a "new" dress that fit even though she had grown 3" since last year. Boys wore pants made from dad's old overcoat, etc.

Gasoline quickly became unavailable for private cars. As the NS and the German military took control of Norway, most private cars were confiscated by the NS and ordered to serve as taxis and doctor transports. With gasoline being unavailable, cars, buses and trucks were powered by wood gas generators. In Norway they were mostly called generators, I'll use WGG here. Most WGGs for buses and trucks were cylinder shaped, 18" diameter and 6' height, and had to be placed vertically. Often a big piece of the vehicle body had to be cut out. Pipes about 2" wide had to be built from the WGG to the engine compartment. These vehicles were permanently damaged. After the war most of them had to be welded together to be used for a while. After all, cars were rationed in Norway till 1960. To get the vehicles started, the WGG had to be fired up. That could take 5-10 minutes. It was also desirable to use a little bit of gasoline to get the WGG-powered engine to start. The wood was called *knott,* chips, and was mostly dry alder or aspen cut to pieces of 2-3". Not only were these WGG vehicles hard to start, but they moved very slowly.

The buses were mostly of a "combined" type. The front half was for passengers, the rear for goods, including mail. The daily ritual for children and young adults was to assemble outside the post office and wait for the bus. Then wait for the mail to be sorted. The mail contained the weekly magazines, and included some children's magazines too. The next bus stop was the stores. The "nice" bus drivers let us kids ride on the bus the last ¼ mile to the store. This was often the last stop. We figured out quickly which bus driver was nice and who was not.

It was not just lack of gas that was troubling the bus traffic. Spare parts were almost impossible to come by. And we lived about 80 km from the bus garage. Such a thing as tow trucks were nonexistent, problems had to be fixed right then and there. I remember one time the bus driver had to stop over for repair in our community when he showed us a contraption made out of wood. This served as the wheel spring for the bus from Hovden to Valle. The driver had made it himself.

The war time was stressful, and more so as people were tired of the war. This created fertile ground for looking to God for help. Valle had two "churches," the main Statskirken, and Frikirken, the Free Church. Frikirken in Valle had been established in 1929 largely in protest to one of my father's predecessors who showed too much understanding and accommodation towards the secular youth. In other words, Frikirken started as a more conservative church. Frikirken in Valle joined a statewide, but not state controlled, "Den Evangelisk Lutherske Frikirke." The establishment of Frikirken had in the 1920s caused a lot of community conflict. Valle was a very religious community, and the religious people took their faith very seriously. The conflict was profound and affected neighbors and families. In some cases it even resulted in mental breakdowns, with some people being hospitalized for a while.

By the time the war started, the church battle had subsided as an open battle. Frikirken was established, but membership did not increase much. Everybody else belonged to Statskirken, whether active or not. In Valle there were no other churches. Adults would seldom attend the other church, but kids would sometimes go to both churches, such as attending Sunday school and the *Juletrefest*, the Christmas Church Party.

During the last two years of the war, Valle received two pastors, one from Frikirken and one from Statskirken. They were not there simultaneously, but both conducted religious awakening meetings over a period of 2-3 months. Their meetings attracted a lot of young people, but also children. There was a lot of enthusiasm and conversions. I remember my parents were concerned about such intense evangelization towards children, but there was not really anything that could be done. And nothing was done to stop it. After a few more months the war was over, and the "new converts" were back in their "sinful" ways.

Immediately after the war ended, the Resistance Movement guys, known as *Hjemmefronten,* the Home Front, came literally "out of the woods." There were no German soldiers in Valle when the war ended, but there were many NS members. The order was to arrest everyone who was an NS member. All NS members were to assemble at the City Hall, for later to be transported farther south where a jail could be found. The NS men—I don't remember any woman being among the arrested in Valle— were a quiet, subdued group. During the war there had been whispers that the NS members would be interned at Björnöya, a small uninhabited island in the Arctic north of Norway. How serious that idea had been, I don't know, but no jail was actually built there.

My father was appointed temporary mayor. Schools were shut down and the NS teachers were fired. It was May, so schools were due to be out soon anyway. And the teachers, who at that time were all men, were arrested. The flags came out. That was such a big deal because flags had been hidden during the war in protest against the NS.

The first day of peace, on May 8, there was a parade through the village. I cannot remember, but I assume there was a lot of singing of "Ja, vi elsker," and other nationalistic and Christian songs. There was a lot of "Thank God" in the air.

On May 17, the National Holiday, there was naturally a parade. But there was also a troop of Home Front soldiers, who had by now got their arm bands with Norwegian flags. Our heroes! Present were also some Scottish soldiers in kilts. For us 12-year-old boys, that was more shocking than anything we had ever seen. Men wearing skirts! Pleated skirts! This must be the end of the world! And the Home Front guys had fireworks. Wow, was that something after years of darkness with covered windows! There is no 4th of July in Portland that can match the excitement of the fireworks in Valle on May 17, 1945.

The Germans had more helpers than the NS during the war. There were a number of people who profiteered from working for the NS. Such work was mostly paid in cash. The new Norwegian government decided to replace the currency. All cash had to be exchanged at a local point, probably a bank. Effective September 10, 1945, the old bank notes would no longer be legal tender. This is how the new government would find and punish the profiteers. Not everybody exchanged their cash. Some people would rather forfeit their money than having it be official knowledge. For several years after the war, "old" money was a nightmare for bank tellers; "old" money was intermingled with the new. When Dad became temporary mayor in Valle, his office had a big safe. I remember he had to keep overnight one or two sacks of "invalidated" cash in his office.

The "prisoners" came home. One of the teachers was met by a well-to-do man, with a somewhat shady war reputation, who wanted to shake his hand. The teacher refused demonstratively. There were a lot of people present.

The favorite games after the war was "Home Front & Nazis." Boys only. Guns were homemade, were used as symbols only. Pointing the gun at someone and screaming: "You are dead!" was enough to declare a winner. The most popular boys were always Home Front, the less likable were Nazis. Somehow the Home Front boys always won. The vicarage barn was great for these war games. It was spring, and the barn was mostly empty. It was a superior playground. In the 1970s some little boys accidentally set fire to the barn. It burned completely to the ground and was never rebuilt. It makes me sad. It is like half of my childhood home is gone.

You could every so often hear people talk after the war, saying those who died were the lucky ones. This sentiment was mostly heard about the merchant marine sailors. The survivors were not treated fairly after the war, said many. There were also many alcoholics after the war. Many of these had been involved in the Resistance Movement, but also many had served with the Germans on the Eastern Front. Nowadays we talk about Post Traumatic Stress Disorder. Then there was no label, and no treatment. Now there is a label, PTSD, but I wonder if there is any better treatment now.

I knew, or knew of, four men from Valle who were sent to concentration camps in Germany. Two of these were young brothers and students. They died there. Another survived, said later that he survived only because some Christian fellow prisoner helped him. He later served in the Norwegian parliament. The fourth was discovered outside the barracks, in the body pile by the Allied soldiers. Then there was Knut Bö. He had been the leader of a Resistance group and was severely tortured before he was shot and buried in the Trandum forest in Norway.

The South of Norway had their No. 1 Gestapo helper: Ole Wehus. He was from Kristiansand and worked for the Gestapo at Arkivet in Kristiansand. He was considered so brutal that even the German Gestapo officers had to restrain him sometimes. Arkivet in Kristiansand—a Gestapo HQ during the war—is now turned into a very authentic Gestapo museum where mannequins are dressed as bloodied prisoners, while the actual tools of torture are preserved there. Then there are pictures and descriptions of each of the German Gestapo officers and Ole Wehus, who for some reason was sent through Valle after the war, supposedly needed for some court case. Some of my friends got to see him. They thought he looked so nice. Ole Wehus was sentenced to death and executed in 1947.

All the German Gestapo officers at Arkivet were arrested and sentenced to life in prison by the new Norwegian court. They were all pardoned in 1953; in other words, the German Gestapo officers served only eight years in prison, and certainly not in a concentration camp prison.

Chapter 3: Western Norway

KARI'S STORY: BERGEN, 1940-1945
by Astri Grieg Fry

This story reflects my mother's views, as expressed during my growing up years, of the Nazi occupation of Norway. Although World War II was an exceedingly grim era, my parents were nonetheless fortunate. They were young and the Nazis did not take anyone close to them. After I wrote the first draft in 1995, my father contributed some details of his own, expressing considerable surprise at what I had remembered.

In the spring of 1940, I, Kari Hedenstad, was twenty-two. I was a nursing student, and I had become engaged. Life was exciting and full of promise. I was assigned to a hospital in Bergen, the hometown of Odd Milne Grieg, my handsome fiancé.

9 April, 1940. What had been the merest speculation has now become ghastly reality. German forces have invaded Norway. Like many other areas, Bergen was occupied in just a few hours, thanks to the readiness of several German cargo ships full of soldiers and weaponry. Odd's uncle, as the commander of the Bergen garrison, had the dubious "honor" of being relieved of his command by the German Wehrmacht officers. Our royal family and government are fleeing to safety to England via Northern

123

Norway, and patriotic Norwegian express their shock and outrage at this violation of our sovereignty and neutrality. I'm glad that the royal family escaped from the German invasion. (I've never liked the coincidence that the entire Russian Tsar family was brutally shot to death the night of 16-17 July, 1918— just hours after I was born!)

17 May, 1940. Over the radio, we listened as our patriotic family poet, Nordahl Grieg, broadcast his Syttende Mai poem (*translated by Astri Grieg Fry*):

> *On this day, our flagpole stands bare*
> *among Eidsvold's greening trees,*
> *But precisely in this hour*
> *we know the meaning of freedom.*
> *A song arises throughout the land,*
> *victorious in its lyrics,*
> *Albeit whispered through compressed lips,*
> *while under the yokes of strangers.*

This spring, Odd and others made their way over the mountains to Voss to join the Norwegian forces based there. German airplanes bombed the area. After only a few weeks, all overt Norwegian resistance collapsed, and Odd and other civilians returned home.

Months have passed and I no longer feel any joy in my work. Under this enforced Nazi rule, everyone is expected to work. For women, one exception is to get married, but we can't afford it yet as Odd is still a college student. I am young and normally in excellent health, but I am beginning to lose weight. As a nursing student, I am on my feet from morning till night. The older nurses keep us young ones on the go, and the night shifts are very tiring.

More months have passed. It is impossible for me to forget about the war as my duties now include attending to German soldiers. Their *Führer's* specter haunts us. His picture is displayed prominently in the ward, but I found a measure of comic relief yesterday. With the most innocent expression I could muster, I pointed at Hitler's picture and, in my best high school German, asked a patient about the subject's identity: *"Wer ist das?"* My patient turned red with anger, but fortunately his casts kept him immobilized in bed as I beat a hasty retreat back to the safety of the Nurses' Station.

Winter 1941-42. I ride the streetcar back and forth to work. At the rear of the streetcar is an open, outside area. Whenever German soldiers board, all who are able leave their sheltered seats, choosing instead to stand at the back, exposed to the frigid temperatures. Such action is no longer tolerated by the current regime. Now we must remain in our seats, regardless of any Nazi presence. Resistance to these unpopular Germans has therefore become more subtle. They have not yet caught onto the fact that a paper clip displayed on a Norwegian's collar or lapel is a sign of national unity. For people who strut about posing as "Masters of the Universe," they are in some ways very dense. Take, for example, their sense of humor—they provide footnotes explaining the punch line of every joke! Give me the Norwegians or the British any day!

Reading the newspapers is an exercise in futility. It's all German propaganda. It has become mandatory to hand radios over to the Germans, but Odd chose instead to conceal our radio behind the hall paneling. This is a highly illegal activity to engage in, risking capital punishment if caught. Thanks to his resourcefulness, we have been able to pick up the BBC news from London, an entirely different point of view! However, much of it is very distressing. There are reports that the Germans have burned entire Norwegian settlements where the population has been suspected of concealing members of our Underground Movement. Also, acts of sabotage by the Underground have caused the Germans to retaliate by taking innocent civilians as hostages and then shooting them. In addition are the rumors of people being deported to concentration camps on the slightest of charges. We hardly know what to think these days!

3 September, 1942. Today is my wedding day. I have been able to sew my own gown, otherwise I don't know where I could have bought one.

The war motto of "Guns instead of butter" does little to inspire Norwegian morale. We are the targets of foreign aggression. The Nazis systematically are taking everything, and what little we are allotted is of inferior quality.

Autumn 1943. Since graduating from college, Odd has been working here in Bergen for an Oslo company. I quit working at last, as I am expecting our first child. I feel worn out from working during this war and from subsisting on inadequate food rations. I want to have a family of my own, but what sort of a world am I bringing this child into?

Odd Milne Grieg and Kari Hedenstad
on their wedding day, 3 September, 1942

May 1944. Our daughter, Eva, was born in March. She was two weeks overdue, as if reluctant to come into this precarious world. Because of the baby's allotted food rations, we are faring better and even have milk again!

There isn't much to laugh about these days, but yesterday I had to, in spite of myself. My mother-in-law, that well-meaning, domineering soul, stopped by our apartment, announcing, "Now that you have *three* ration cards, you should *absolutely* share your food with me, as I have only *one* card to my name!" The fact that we have three mouths to feed seemed to escape her notice. I stopped by our church today to register for Eva's christening, and today happens to be Syttende Mai, 1944. That date used to be our Constitution Day, jubilantly celebrated. Now it is just another day.

The war in Europe ended on 8 May, 1945. There still were hundreds of thousands of German combat troops occupying Norway. However, by this time, even the Germans couldn't stomach any more war, but surrendered. I will say this for them: they withdrew in an orderly fashion—in our area at least—although they had made a wasteland out of Northern Norway. Syttende Mai that year was celebrated as never before! The following year, our second daughter was born. With no time to reach the hospital, Astri was delivered at home with the assistance of a neighbor and a green-faced taxi driver—two weeks early. This time, however, the arriving infant seemed confident that the world once again had become a safe and welcoming place!

AASE HEDENSTAD: A HIGH SCHOOL STUDENT IN ODDA AND BERGEN

by Aase Alstad and Astri Grieg Fry

The war? I remember April 1940 as clearly as if it were yesterday! I was on my bicycle, coming from my home in Odda, when from Byrkjanes a long column of foreign soldiers advanced, singing as they marched—in OUR land! The effect was instantaneous: I shook my fist at them as I cycled past, tears streaming down my face, but the Germans continued singing without missing a beat. After that I decided that they should feel my eternal hatred and contempt!

Later, when attending Katedralskolen in Bergen with the long walk home to Årstadveien 15, I, along with others, would encounter more soldiers occasionally. They advanced marching and singing as before, and one my friends proposed: "Stuff your fingers in your ears!" The Germans paid us no attention, which was just as well. However, occasionally we came across some German women, staying near us at Stadsarkivet (an official archival building, now requisitioned by the Germans), just past my in-law Mrs. Grieg's house. When they ventured forth in groups of two or three, we unceremoniously ordered them out of the way: "Gehen Sie mir aus dem Wege, bitte!" and strode past, noses in the air. Insulted, they shouted back at us, but what did we care, feeling only they deserved to be treated rudely by us—whether or not that really was true!

But then there was that summer vacation at home in Odda when my friend Inger and I were going to Gangdal to shop. The Germans came marching and singing as always, from the Skogly Pond. OUR pond! In their swimsuits! Then I plugged my ears once too often. An imbecile of a soldier came running and babbled about "Finger in den Ohren." Yes, I understood his German sufficiently and had to go with him. En route the numbskull tried to explain to me the error of my ways. An officer who arrived on the scene, took charge and admonished against entertaining the lady, "Ach, du brauchst die Dame nicht unterhalten!" A most unpleasant situation, of course. The Germans lived at the local school, and so I had to go along to the teachers' Lounge, where I had never been before. The officer wanted to see my ID card. I never carried it with me. That day my brother-in-law Lodin had it, and he was somewhere else entirely. The officer wanted to know how this could be possible. German thoroughness!! "Durch einen Zufall," I shrugged, trotting out my best high school German— merely by coincidence. Then I was on the receiving end of a blistering lecture. Once it died down, I ventured, "Sie brauchen die Dame nicht unterhalten!"—echoing what I had heard before. Then I have to admit, he could take a joke. A more superior officer was called over, and he actually was all right too. He used a term that was new to me: *provokation,* which I made a mental note of; however, I got out of there before having to promise to mend my ways. My father heard about this incident and came from his office, and in faulty German accused the Germans of

130

dragging his daughter from the place: "Ich höre jetzt das meine Tochter ausgeschleppt ist." "Wer hat das getan!" they roared, demanding to know how that could have happened. Once he understood that I had been released in a routine manner, this misunderstanding was cleared up. Whew!

Two days later a police officer named Holm came to get me. I was going to jail; my mother and I parted at the jail cell door. The guard's wife gave me tea and sandwiches for supper, and what a treat that was! The next day I was pardoned and again released. But not exactly feeling more docile.

In another instance, the guard at "Neset" demanded IDs constantly whenever we passed by, which, as mentioned, I neglected to carry on my person. "Heute habe ich leider keine Pass," I answered often. Kalle, as he was called, finally just let me pass, although hoping my return would be impeded, "Sie können passieren, aber zurück kommen Sie nicht!" This was no idle threat. The road along the fjord there overlooked some sheer cliffs. But we were going to Stana, and from there, there was a mountain trail along a steep and spectacular terrain, with a 1000 meter difference in elevation. It was September and sunny. Because of the cliffs and the curfew, I now had a pretext not to come back the same way, because I actually was not allowed to hike alone in the mountains. My friend Gudny had told Kalle at Neset on her return earlier that I had gone to Stana and was afraid to return. "Gut, zurück kommt sie nicht!" said he as usual—"Ha! Ha! Ha!"—clearly hoping for the worst, given the terrain. But he hoped in vain. It was a long hike for me before I finally did come back from the roundabout direction. My mother was not exactly pleased, but that was mostly because I had worn down her hiking boots on that long trek, which was indeed regrettable. Almost as bad was the fact that I was wearing my older sister Ingeborg's navy blue silk blouse, tailored for her narrower shoulders. With me perspiring like mad while hiking, the blouse had split open clear down the back. Ingeborg could on occasion be a wonderful older sister. She took this mishap in stride, especially considering we had to share each other's clothes during the war.

Another problem during these years was the lack of food. We never had enough to eat. A classmate of mine lived at Os, and I was happy to ride my bike 30 km there as often as possible. We would have a wonderful supper, then 30 km back again, but at least on a full stomach!

A brighter side during this time, was that the unity between students and teachers was fabulous. I was expelled once for two months as a result of my overly impulsive behavior, but it was thanks to a teacher, Trygve Bull, that I was allowed to return to school. Meanwhile, on the less bright side, our principal Stoltz had been incarcerated in the Oslo prison Grini, and now we had a Nazi principal. One of the teachers, our religion teacher, became a Nazi. After that his real name wasn't even used anymore, not even by his fellow teachers, just his nickname "Prayerman." Eventually our former principal returned home and could be seen ambling around in the vicinity of his beloved school. One day Inger Johanne and I met him during a long recess. We dropped him a deep curtsey, of course. He asked about the new principal. "We only refer to him as the man in the principal's office," answered Inger Johanne. "It was "Prayerman" who informed on me," said principal Stoltz. In February 1942 when the teachers went on strike, all instruction ceased and the school closed. I was about to return home to Odda. Our English teacher, Finn Glambæk, gave me assignments that I could write and mail to him, and he would correct them. That worked fine until we got the news that he had been sent to the Kirkenes camp in Northern Norway along with many other teachers. When we learned that, we wept. When he returned much later, he had lost a finger.

In 1941 my friend Inger Johanne and I were studying for our orals in geology. The hours had passed and turned into days, and we were making no progress whatsoever. We lived at some distance from each other and agreed to meet somewhere downtown. This actually was a poor idea, as it was impossible to find any place where we could study in peace and quiet. Moreover, we had to be home well before nine every night. The Germans had established this curfew, that is to say: a curfew applying to Norwegians. Other people might be arrested and interned for staying out too late at night, but we did not feel that this restriction applied to us in any way, of course! However, we began feeling really discouraged as our geology grades now hung in the balance. Maybe we should risk internment —surely we would survive one such awful night? We met as agreed, but then, with plummeting spirits, we procrastinated about our return home. We tried to console each other that we probably would not have to take the oral exam once we had spent the night in jail. When there was barely a half hour left before the hour of nine, we reached a joint decision: HOME! Each of us raced homeward, en route I sprinted by the Town Gate, Hansa, Kalfaret—finally Årstadveien was in view! Just then a truck started from nearby Stadsarkivet, took off, and stopped just opposite Årstadveien 15, and a German soldier jumped off the back of the truck. I can still see how his knees absorbed the shock of his descent. But I reached the gate, tore it open, rushed in and closed it! Then I blessed the German who meanwhile had his back to me, as I was absolutely terrified!

My high school years in Bergen during the war were chaotic, but never boring. Those were indeed unique times!

WORLD WAR II MEMORIES
FROM STAVANGER, NORWAY, 1940-1945
by Johanna Borrevik Fedde

On 8 April, 1940, we arrived home after a ski trip. I was a 21-year-old student at Oslo University. The University Square was quite full of students who were reading newspapers with great interest. The British had laid mines down in several places in the western fjords. In the evening I read in the window displays of the prominent newspapers that a ship full of young German men, all dressed alike, had stranded outside the southern town of Lillesand (where my mother grew up). The population there had flocked together and helped the young men, many wounded, away from the ship and to the shore to get medical aid.

I went home and to bed. But about 12 o'clock the signal sounded, and we had to take shelter in the cellar and remain until the next signal meant the danger was over. I lived in a big apartment building, and the cellar was made ready for many people who crowded in to the room. We heard rumors that there was fighting outside the small towns in Oslofjorden. About 6 or 7 o'clock a.m. people became impatient when they heard no "danger over" signal and they left for their apartments. I decided to join my student friends at the pension near St. Hanshaugen. At the crossing between Drammensveien and the Oslo University, I discovered quite a big group of German soldiers marching into the city's center. These were the first occupation troops. I hurried on to St. Hanshaugen. There my friends were seated in the living room of the third floor watching some airplanes, German and Norwegian, shooting at each other. My friends seemed unaware of the danger. When that was over, we discussed the best thing to do. We had to get money to be able to travel home, away from Oslo. The leader of Studiehjemmet, the Study House, loaned us the money to take the railway to Kristiansand and then to take the train from Flekkefjord to Stavanger, my hometown.

We managed to get as far as Kristiansand. But here the train stopped. I noticed that the spire of the church had been shot down. I said to a German soldier, "Look what you have done!" He appeared somewhat ashamed and disappeared. During the first days Germany sent nicer soldiers, later on they sent the rougher kind. After a few minutes the soldier returned with a loaf of German black bread. First we did not know if we should accept it. But we knew food would be hard to get when communications were breaking down. Later that day we shared the bread with some Norwegian naval soldiers, whose ship had been sunk near Arendal. They had to walk to Flekkefjord. We, four girls, also began walking. A Norwegian truck driver stopped and got us on board his truck. But our trip lasted only about five minutes. Then a German patrol stopped us and said they needed the truck. After some time another Norwegian truck took us up, but German soldiers confiscated this one too. We walked on with our rucksacks. In front of us we noticed about six naval soldiers. They said they could *på staten*, by courtesy of the government, order a bus or truck. A bus driver said he was willing to obey the

136

Norwegian soldiers. We shared a meal on the bus and when we discovered a bakery, the soldiers said they could let the "state" give us a little more, maybe some bread and cookies. When we drove on, we noticed several buses full of young men. They were going to war, but first stopping at various places to register and get more soldiers aboard.

The Central Hotel in Flekkefjord had two rooms for us. But first we had to go by the postmaster's to deliver greetings from his daughter. The postmaster's old aunt was visiting there and said, "We have no German soldiers here. They won't find us here at the end of the fjord. And should they still come here, we will sound the church bells!"

The next morning we got the last train to Stavanger for a long time. It was evacuation day in Stavanger and the streets were mostly empty. My parents were waiting for me. Our house was next to an old Viking mound and while my father and friends stood on the top of the mound to look toward Sola Airport, a burning plane without steering flew at a low height over the mound and fell down about five blocks away with explosions and ignitions, destroying the Storhaug School. The school was not rebuilt until quite a while after the war. We had to run across the street to take shelter at a neighbor's place, with a better air raid room than we had. There were peculiar colored signals in the sky. An aunt began talking of the last days of the world.

The next morning we saw German soldiers being stationed at an air gun nest on the top of the mound and they remained there till the end of the war. Stavanger was lucky, though, and did not have any worse accidents. Once

I read in the newspaper that a German plane had lightened its load and let a bomb drop near Hillevags Vatnet. Hearing the address, my friend said, "But that is my home!" A big stone flew up from the garden and landed through a broken window on the pillow of her stepfather Rector Olden's bed. My friend told me he was not at home. He had previously been arrested and was at Grini Concentration Camp (the big camp outside Oslo) and strictly guarded.

While in Oslo I saw two accidents. I was swimming at "Katten" in Oslofjorden. From there I saw a big explosion in Oslo Harbor. Some ammunition ships exploded and traffic had to be redirected. We were all on bicycles because there was no gasoline for cars. The other time I was sitting on the sofa in front of the big windows at Studiehjemmet, when some planes suddenly came into view. They bombed the house where the German S.S. was staying near Drammensveien. But the damage was not great. It was much worse later near Christmas when the *trikk*, or tram, was hit.

The trip between Oslo and Stavanger had to be applied for. Everybody had to have a *grenseboer bevis*, border resident proof, to be allowed to travel. My mother put a string in my *grenseboer bevis* so I could wear it around my neck and not lose it. This was also practical when I went skiing. But when German police were checking, they looked very skeptically at it as if I was dishonest!

From the first days of the war I had to give up my own room on the third floor and spend the nights on a couch on the first floor. It was too dangerous to spend so much time on the stairs if we had an alarm. I was awakened every night at about 1 o'clock by airplanes taking off to go bomb England. It was the time when the Germans marched in the streets singing, "Denn wir fahren gegen England." Then they came back about 4 o'clock waking us again. No alarm. We just missed our quiet sleep.

My father had now made a safer place in our cellar in case of a longer alarm period spent. Once we had to run head over heels downstairs and hide under tables in the laundry cellar. But God held his hand over us and all the while we were sitting as next-door neighbors to the machine gun nest on the Viking hill. Fortunately, nothing wrong happened to our house. The worst damage was when we had three days' snow and children used our sleds to go from the top of the mound and run into our white garden fence. That gave father hard repair work to do.

On our first 17th of May (Norway's Constitution Day) since the war began, we celebrated with coffee in the garden. Then suddenly a girl came up the street teasing a soldier to run down from his watch on the top of the mound to talk to her. My mother put down her coffee cup and hurried over to them. She reminded the girl that we never must speak to the Germans. The girl just laughed and probably made the soldier understand what mother was saying. He got angry and showed his gun. We all got scared and shouted to mother that she should back off from there. We drank the rest of our coffee, an experience richer!

The schools were closed from the first days of the war. The teachers were sent to do other kinds of work. My father, a teacher from the burnt-out Storhaug School, was told to watch an air raid shelter room during the daytime and keep it secure. An uncle of mine, also a teacher, was told to go about counting hens, as people began keeping hens, helping the food situation with their eggs. My mother got remnants of bread thrown out at a hospital, as food for the hens. She could provide eggs for two or three families.

The Storhaug School remained a skeletal structure until after the war. I think the reason no attempt was made to rebuild the school was because the Norwegians knew the Germans would only occupy it. After a while both food and clothing were getting scarce. Instead of leather soles we had to buy shoes with wooden soles. It sounded as if the town were full of wooden shoes tramping along! If people had cars, these had to be saved for better times. Old bicycles were used in traffic. The Germans used big trucks and they could be dangerous for children and bicycles. I had a pen friend in Germany before the war. After the war, when we could write together again, I heard she had been killed by one of these big trucks.

Schools began working again in the fall of 1940. However, all school buildings were used by German soldiers. So the Norwegians had to take private houses and office buildings for classrooms. I had my first year as a practicing teacher. We began at 8 o'clock a.m. For my first class, I ran to a telephone building. After 45 minutes of teaching a class furnished with normal desks, I had 15

140

minutes to find my next class, maybe at a school with the first two floors taken by Germans. The Norwegians were placed on the third floor. They would then risk being the first hit by an attack. Fortunately it never happened. If there were any free minutes left, one could chat with other colleagues and discuss the latest news and rumors. But the newspapers could not be relied upon. Since the earliest days of the war the editors had been changed. Only Nazi opinions could show up in the news. One had to look for real news in the illegal newspapers. One might get great fines and prison time if caught with one of those.

Back to my school day. I might have to spend an hour close to the center of the town. It was an old business and technical school. Sometimes the boys might catch a rat in the schoolyard and put it dead on the master's desk, a great scare for the incoming teacher. From the old technical school I had to run to a chapel at the border of the town. There the students had to sit on benches and write on their knees. Another place was given to a class in a nice district of the city where a family was living. Benches were placed in a music room. A big grand piano was taking up much of the space. When our students were left alone for the 15-minute break, they understood the situation and kept quiet even without any teachers watching.

One day teachers were discussing news and wondering at the absence of a colleague. Could he have been arrested? He suddenly appeared. "I have become a father," he said and offered cigars. Later we were invited to see his wife and baby. They had been billeted with two old ladies in a beautiful house, that after the war was promoted to a museum as a Jugendstyle house (art nouveau). Some of us could then boast that we had already seen it!

As for our food situation, our richer neighbor countries, Denmark and Sweden understood that Norway needed help with food. They sent us soup of oats to serve our school children. Big buckets arrived daily between 10 and 11 a.m. The children brought cups from home and the teachers served it into their cups. It could be quite heavy work and sometimes you might feel like sliding on the floor. Once I heard a child's voice say, "Teacher, you have soup in your hair."

After four hours, at 12 o'clock the school day was over for those who started at 8 a.m. The next group of students arrived at noon. Midday the whole town smelled of fried herring, which saved us from starving. For a variety, we sometimes lined up to buy a variation of fishcakes made of a white kind of shark about one meter long. It tasted very much like those made from codfish. The 12 o'clock children stayed in school until 4 o'clock. Then there was an hour for dinner, and the older students came to school at 5 o'clock and then back home between 8 and 9 p.m. This shortened school day was because the Germans had occupied all the school buildings and the Norwegians were short of classrooms.

The Germans wanted to force Nazi dogmas on the schools, but were not successful. Teachers resisted, often with humor. Once the Nazis tried to enlist all school children into a Nazi organization. The schools then pushed all registers out of order and the teachers hid their lists of names. I hid my registers under the henhouse. They were immaculate when we gave them back again to the administration.

A bad blow to Norwegian schools was in early 1942, when the Nazis arrested several hundreds of teachers. They spent some days in prison. Then they stayed for a while in Oslo, in Grini concentration camp. Then sent by train, some in open freight cars to Trondheim. From there they were sent by ship to a concentration camp near Kirkenes. One ship was overfilled with nearly 500 where there should only be about 250. My father, in Stavanger, was hauled out of bed and taken to prison. He was about 60 years old. At Kirkenes he was put to work on a road. Others, younger ones, were loading or unloading ships. One or two lost their lives because of falling into the hull of a ship.

Some students were also sent away. One day the police came to the university and swept through the reading rooms taking male students. They were put in the cellar for the night and then shipped to the German concentration camp near Weimar. Also at night they came through the student homes full of girls and two of my friends were among those taken.

After a while the Germans seemed to show some respect for the teachers. The soldiers had gone to school in Germany where a teacher was a respected person. Once in a while the soldiers discussed problems and asked the opinion of a Norwegian teacher. Some of the Germans had admiration for the Norwegian schools and their culture.

In the meantime Norwegian schools suffered greatly. Eventually, German and Norwegian Nazis began to think Norwegian schools had suffered enough. The 60-year-olds were sent home from Kirkenes after six months and the whole camp after eight months. They were living in tents with snow around. My father and an uncle were very lean when they arrived home, but they seemed to have suffered no lasting damage. The trip at sea was no joke, though. The crowded ship became the goal of Russian bombardment. The Russians (then Soviets) had not received the news that the Norwegian German ship was freighting the Norwegian teachers. It went well, however. After a short time the Norwegian schools were doing better, even though teachers continued every hour to run between different addresses. But after the war the German language lost its important position in the Norwegian foreign language curriculum. When I went to school the first foreign language I learned was German. After the war this changed.

One early fall day, a Saturday, I went to visit a friend to hear news. She was working for an illegal newspaper. To my great surprise a policeman opened the door for me and ordered me to enter. My friend came downstairs with a policeman. They were going down to Strøket in Stavanger, the downtown area where young people gathered after work, from about 5 to 7 p.m. The police wanted to see if anybody there sought to contact my

144

friend. I had to stay under the watch of a young policeman. I decided not to irritate him and rather to act young and stupid. I asked about the insignia on his uniform. I tried to be friendly and curious. The young policeman thought I must be rather silly when I said it would be interesting to be questioned. "It is not interesting at all," he said. And when the senior policeman returned, he said, "She knows nothing. No use trying. She can leave."

I felt very lucky and bicycled to an uncle at the other end of the town so the police would not find me so easily if they changed their mind. I found out from the questions of my young watchman that a young man I had met there the day before had killed another young man and then killed an important Nazi living in the same house. Two days later my friend did not show up at a party. She had been arrested. In the eastern part of Stavanger all grown men were called away from home and were taken to a schoolyard in their nightclothes. They sang Christmas songs to keep warm. In the morning they were allowed to go home. They were all made to suffer for the murder of the Nazi. My friend and her sister were sent to Grini Concentration Camp because they had sheltered the murderer. Fortunately I had not known any thing about it.

By now war was going worse for the Germans in Russia and Europe. The Jewish synagogue had its place right below Studiehjemmet in Oslo. Now Jews were gathered there from the whole country to be sent to concentration camps in Germany and occupied countries, but no news of this came to us until several days later. Even

145

when news reached us there was never anything about it in the newspapers!

In Stavanger all Jews were caught. A German Nazi had an apartment in the house of the Jewish owner of a well-known 10-cent store. The German had been his friend, then suddenly they were enemies and the Nazi got rid of the Jewish family in the house: the man, his wife and two nephews. Only one nephew survived until the end of the war. He was afraid of being caught even after the war. He moved away from Stavanger and then took another name.

Finally, around the end of April 1945, there were strong rumors that the war was over. It must have been when Hitler committed suicide, but it was not verified. About a week or so later I was called to our next-door neighbor and asked to listen to a German radio message. In 1941 radios had been handed in and forbidden to be used. It was a German general's message that Germany had given up the war. It was the 7th of May, my father's 60th birthday, but my parents asked me to go and find out what was happening in the town. I found three friends making their way to town and joined them. It was like the whole town was gathering in the market place. Happy faces everywhere! We passed the little prison of Stavanger. There the doors were opened and the first political prisoners were let out, looking rather confused. In the main street, Kirkegaten, people had gotten into Nazi offices and were throwing down papers and documents out of the windows. It was like wading through snow when we walked through Kirkegaten.

146

The next day it was almost the same celebration. The 8th of May was considered the day of peace. A British company of soldiers came marching into our marketplace, with long steps and arms swinging. A few places we noticed young men with scissors ready to cut the hair of girls who had been friendly with German soldiers. Hair was gathering in the ditches of the streets. But I don't think this was tolerated once the police saw it.

In the evening there were fireworks in the marketplace. It seemed to be the same sights as we had the first days of the war, at the bombing accident. They were probably burning up some of the German signs and signals. However, we could not yet count on security—the Germans were still armed. When a girl was approached by someone that tried to cut her hair, her German boyfriend swung his gun and the crowd suddenly took off from the center of the marketplace. But we walked safely home.

I moved back to my own room on the third floor. Now I would sleep soundly all night! However, I awoke at 1 o'clock. I thought I heard a cannon shooting. No, it couldn't be! It sounded like a thunderstorm. I settled for that and had the first quiet night of peace on May 8, 1945.

I had a class of 13-year-old girls at the Free Church. We kept school open on Saturday and were on the second floor when a girl suddenly called out, "Look there!" A whole bridal procession came riding bicycles, as they couldn't obtain any cars. We almost broke out singing, "A bicycle built for two." My class could see and hear through chinks in the walls and floors, and I had to let them listen.

It was the best Saturday entertainment. Afterward, the wedding party disappeared for a bridal lunch, transported on their bicycles.

Another day we had a visit from British soldiers. During the break they came over to try the schoolgirls' English. We invited them into the classroom upstairs, and with good help, they managed to understand some of what the British soldiers could tell them of their life across the North Sea. With the war lasting five years, there had been no chance for 13-year-olds to travel abroad, and it became a good memory for the class.

Finally by the fall of 1945 schools were working more smoothly, the lack of housing was improved and we no longer lived with Nazi guns on the Viking mound next door.

KAARE NIELSEN MEMORIES
by Kaare and Joyce Nielsen

Kaare was born and raised in Sand, Ryfylke, in Rogaland, Norway; a small town not far from Stavanger. When he was sixteen years old, he was doing his Maritime Schooling on board the *Statsraad Lehmkuhl*, a sailing vessel whose home port is Bergen. The ship was in England in 1939, and they were anticipating a trip across the Atlantic to the United States when the British entered the war against Germany, and the ship returned to Bergen. Kaare immediately returned to his home in Sand.

On April 9, 1940 the Germans invaded Norway. Before the Germans arrived in Sand, Kaare and his father had removed the wheels and tires from their car. They also removed a few other parts that were essential to the car running. The tires and parts were then taken to his uncle Nicholai's flour mill, where they were effectively hidden. When asked by the Germans what had happened to the car, they were told the car had stopped running and the wheels, tires, and parts had been sold. Other Norwegians living in the area were not as lucky, as the Germans confiscated every car they found. Kaare and a cousin were down at the dock one day and were able to take pictures of some of the cars before they were loaded on a ship and sent to Germany. Those cars were never seen in Sand again, but Kaare still has pictures of them.

Above: Kaare and Nielsen family car
Below: Kaare with a 1935 Ford, later confiscated by the
Germans

When the war was over, the first Norwegian-owned car seen on the streets of Sand was the one owned by Kaare's father. They proudly drove through Sand, honking the horn and displaying the Norwegian flag. During the years of occupation, the Norwegians were not allowed to show their flag.

Kaare's Uncle Bernhardt had a large boat, the *Eagle*, that accommodated 75 passengers. The boat had a regular schedule and ran seven days a week. Kaare worked with his uncle on the boat for several months. It was an important part of the war time economy, as it was a lifeline from Sand to the end of the fjord, taking about four hours either way. The farmers used it to bring milk to Sand and when the fruit ripened, there were tremendous amounts of apples, pears, cherries and plums brought into town. In addition to produce, the farmers also brought cows, horses, goats and sheep with them. It was also a chance for them to buy whatever was available in town. The boat also hauled the mail.

At the beginning of the war, the boat was used to haul Norwegian soldiers and ammunition, and Kaare was on board with his uncle. There was a small town in the fjord where the soldiers disembarked and then hiked over the mountains to where the Norwegian Army was taking a stand against the Germans. Of course that only lasted a week or two.

All Norwegians were expected to work during the war years. At one time Kaare was taken to the steel mill in Sauda (originally a Norwegian-US company), and helped keep the fires going. Of course the Germans erected fences around the factory so the workers were confined. Kaare tells us that at least he was warm while feeding the fires. However, he remembers the food was very sparse. He eventually left the factory, just walking away and able to ride home to Sand on a boat.

He also was sent to Stavanger at one time to work on what the locals call "Hitler's teeth," which are triangular shaped and made out of concrete. Many Norwegian men were put to work constructing these up and down the Norwegian coast. The Germans thought the "teeth" along with deep trenches would effectively disable any tanks if the British should try to land along the Norwegian coast. Some of the "teeth" can still be seen along the coast west of Stavanger.

One of Kaare's sisters was an operator at the telephone exchange and told about having a German soldier on duty there at all times monitoring the telephone calls. Another sister was quite young when Sand was occupied and remembers a soldier in their school room. The teachers were closely monitored as to what they could teach.

The hotel in Sand was originally owned by Kaare's grandfather, but he died shortly before the occupation. It was then managed by Kaare's father on behalf of the family. The German officers occupied the hotel, and it was known throughout the town that the basement was where they questioned suspicious citizens, often using cruelty.

All Norwegian citizens had to carry an identification paper at all times in case they were stopped by authorities. Kaare still has his.

Kaare also delivered mail during the war years, carrying a heavy sack on his back, often skiing to communities outside of Sand. One year it was so cold that fjords froze, and he combined skiing with ice skating as he made his rounds.

Kaare's wartime identification paper

Wherever he went, Kaare had his accordion on his back and often played for dances out in the farming communities. Since they were so far out in the country, the Germans were not aware of the dances.

People were not allowed to be outside after dark, so it was a real challenge in the winter months to keep busy in the evening hours. That was no problem at the Nielsen home, as Kaare's father played accordion, as did Kaare and his brother Arvid. His sister Jenny trained as an opera singer, sister Ruth was an accomplished pianist, as was his sister Maalfrid. As a result of all this talent, music could be heard coming from their house, and the German soldiers liked to gather on the street so they could hear the beautiful melodies being played and sung inside.

The Norwegians were not allowed to listen to the radio, but some of the men in town had managed to hide a radio under the seat of an outhouse. One evening a week they would gather to hear the BBC broadcasts. A neighbor lady could not understand why so many men had to visit the outhouse at the same time. The men were never caught by the Germans.

Another story involved Kaare's Uncle Nicholai who had a room at the hotel where he lived and worked. He managed to take a nap at a certain time when he would listen to his radio, which was hidden from the Germans. One afternoon one of the Germans was looking for him and opened the door to his room. Fortunately Uncle Nicholai was under the covers, and the German commented to another soldier in the hall that he was sleeping, so the door was closed and they left.

Kaare also tells about the day a German ship was being unloaded and a barrel of sauerkraut fell on the dock, spilling its contents. Kaare was there and had no idea what sauerkraut was. All he knew was that it smelled bad. He picked up a nearby pitchfork that had been used for cleaning up manure and moved the smelly stuff back into the barrel before putting the lid back on. He often wondered if the taste had been affected in any way when the Germans enjoyed one of their favorite delicacies.

There were people in Sand who were active in the Underground, but Kaare was too young to be a part of it. After the war, people discovered who they were. One was the veterinarian for the area. He survived the war, and there were many stories to be told about his activities. There were women in the area that had been more than friendly

154

with the occupying forces. After the war they were gathered together and their heads were shaved.

Today Kaare still has many family members living in Sand: primarily children and grandchildren of his cousins. His sister Ruth lived her whole life there until she died in 2014. His younger brother, Arvid, moved to Stavanger when he married. Although Arvid died several years ago, his widow, four children, grandchildren, and great-grandchildren still live there.

Kaare's two younger sisters, Jenny and Maalfrid, on the other hand, both married Americans and moved to the US in the early 1950s. Although they both are now widowed, they live in Aloha and Hillsboro, respectively, not far from Kaare's Beaverton home.

Kaare arrived in Oregon in 1953. In 1954 he went to work at Timberline Lodge where he was their Transportation Manager for ten years. While at Timberline he met and married Alice Oja with whom he had five children. They later divorced.

After leaving Timberline he started his own trucking business, eventually becoming a contract mail contractor with the US Post Office. His business is still operating as K. M. Nielsen Trucking.

Portland Norwegians will remember him playing for dances at Norse Hall. He also accompanied Leikarringen for a while. His group was called Kaare's Trio and they played all over the Portland area for different Scandinavian organizations. He and his trio also traveled to other cities in the Northwest where they played for different Scandinavian events, including the Astoria Midsummer Festival. They also played for dances at the North Portland Eagles for many years as well as other lodges in Portland. Kaare is also remembered for playing his accordion with the popular Midnight Sons who were well known throughout the Northwest.

Kaare and his wife Joyce were married in 1987. She is of Swedish descent. As of this writing, they will soon celebrate their 28th wedding anniversary.

WORLD WAR II IN STAVANGER

by Reidar Gundersen and Astri Grieg Fry

Residing near a military site may not always be an advantage, although at the age of three when the war broke out, I was hardly in any position to judge. Our home was only a ten-minute walk from Byhaugen with its view over the fjord and outlying North Sea. Throughout the war from 1940-45, we often heard firing from the Byhaugen cannons at night. They disturbed whatever sleep I was trying to get in my *ungdomsseng.* This was a two-sectional youth bed which could be extended on demand as its growing occupant acquired length.

Before the war, my parents had lived in the US and my brother was born in Chicago, but they moved back to Norway during the Depression. Since that time, my parents, older brother and I lived in a wooden house with a concrete first floor. Thus this area became our most secure shelter once the Allied attacks began, and these lasted for years. From our home, we could see some German barracks and witnessed first hand the soldiers running to bunkers during air raids. When the Germans conducted war exercises, they varied the locations, but at times they would train behind our house, and invariably the unmistakable sound of their marching feet signaled their approach.

Activities for youngsters were limited during the war and the sudden explosions in our area were unnerving. Nor did new German neighbors inspire trust, as I discovered after our former Norwegian neighbor had been supplanted. Once, while playing in our yard, a ball went over the fence, landing in the yard next door. As I retrieved it, the German officer there gave me the rough side of his tongue. Requisition for the Germans officers' living quarters was determined by the size of the house, and this one had passed muster. Ours, in contrast, was rejected as being too small, although it had not escaped a routine inspection. When the Germans visited us on their unwelcome errand, they didn't bother to ring the doorbell. They simply banged their rifle butts on our front door as their way of announcing their arrival.

Low in the wartime societal pecking order were the Russian prisoners. We saw them serving as domestic slaves to the Germans, and their living quarters were in the basement. When we had the opportunity, we handed them sardine tins and small change. Miserable as their conditions were, these men nevertheless expressed their artistic side. They fashioned rings out of the 50-*øre* coins, copper coins with a hole in the center, or even constructed a toy crocodile out of wood for my brother and me, which wiggled its many moveable joints in a most lifelike manner.

While the German officers took over private homes, the soldiers were quartered in larger buildings such as schools and barracks. In 1944 I started first grade, but the setting offered an exceedingly limited introduction into the academic world. School was held in an old folks' home and during daytime air raids, we spent considerable time in the cellar perched atop a stack of wood. Even once I began attending the local Kampen Skole in 1945, the Nazi

158

presence haunted us still. Swastikas, as their calling cards, were engraved into the wooden door frames.

School lunches consisted of soup out of large milk cans, i.e. a few flakes of oatmeal swimming in a liquid with the hue of gray dishwater. This did nothing for the appetite of a picky eater such as me, and to this day I detest oatmeal. At home, gastronomic prospects were equally limited. The Germans confiscated the cream of the crop—literally—leaving us only with rationed food. My mother often left the house at 4:00 a.m, standing in line for hours hoping to procure a little bit of fish, for example. If the air raids went off during this time, her concern for us left at home alone would be intense. When she could get the ingredients, she would make a paste of flour and oil to spread on our black bread, with a little sugar sprinkled on top so that we would eat it. This spartan diet caused my brother to develop digestive problems, and the doctor prescribed French bread as the cure. When my mother tried to renew this "prescription," she was accused of eating the white bread herself! For a hot beverage, roasted dandelion roots served as a coffee bean substitute. When farmers needed help with the potato harvest, teenagers such as my brother got some potatoes as wages to take home. Unlike us, my grandmother actually had livestock, a pig and some chickens.

With food so hard to come by, it must have been a wrench to leave our *middag,* daily main meal, behind on the table during a mandatory evacuation when I was about four or five. There was an air raid warning, in tandem with a British attack, and we spent several days in Kristianlyst before returning to Stavanger.

My father was a carpenter and very skilled he was too. At one point, the Germans ordered him to the Stavanger airport, Sola, to perform some work for them. He balked, was almost shot by a German lieutenant who stood over him with a pistol at the ready, but just then a higher-ranking officer intervened. That was a close call for Dad!

My uncle and cousin sailed for years in the cargo convoys between New York and England during World War II. The Nazis' treatment of the Norwegians might have reinforced their dedication, as before these relatives decided to leave Norway, they experienced the Germans' confiscation of radios. My cousin was listening to the radio by an open window, whereupon the Germans walked in and cut the radio wires, a dedicated handyman effectively shutting off the live current of 220 volts. After being shot at during the war, my uncle had a steel plate in his leg as a memento. My memento of my uncle was when he returned at the conclusion of the war and presented us with chocolate. My appreciation of this tasty and delightful treat was instantaneous.

Not all family members resisted the German occupiers, however. An uncle on my mother's side was married to a Nazi sympathizer; but eventually he got cold feet, asking himself: "What am I doing?!" He divorced her during the war, and his change of heart did not go unobserved by the German watchdogs. He subsequently went into hiding, in our house, alternating between the attic and the laundry cellar room, until my mother couldn't stand the strain any longer on behalf of our family's safety. He departed around 1943-44; his whereabouts remaining unknown. After the war, both he and his ex-wife were held accountable by the Norwegian authorities, receiving prison sentences. In addition, my aunt was *skamklippet,* shame cut, her hair cut down to the roots. This had become a reactionary post-war practice intended to disgrace publicly those Norwegian women who had fraternized with the enemy.

With everything in such short supply in the wartime years, we once received a care package, and my portion was a pair of boots with wooden soles. When Norway at last was liberated by the Allies in May 1945, the British came to Stavanger and handed out tins of shortbread cookies to the kids. The Norwegian mood by then was jubilant, but my parents wouldn't allow me to go to downtown Stavanger as conditions there were chaotic. No doubt their concern had to do with the presence of thousands of German soldiers still infesting Norway, although these by now were wearing white armbands as a sign of truce and surrender. I had to content myself with having my picture taken in front of our local grocery store along with other neighborhood kids. There were, waving the Norwegian flags out in the open again, after their concealment during the last five years!

One would like to think that the war in Norway ended on the day of the German surrender there, 8 May, 1945, but five years of foreign suppression isn't necessarily shrugged off that instantly. We kids dealt with this in our own way. We explored a burned out troop carrier in our area, marveling at the many hammocks installed in the hold. In addition, foraging around Sola airport, we garnered discarded items like gas masks, cyanide pills in glass vials; spent rifle shells, gunpowder and fuses. With these items we could construct rockets to fire off on the first Syttende Mai to be celebrated after our five long and dark years and shattering a few windows in the process. For someone who had developed a lively aversion to loud and sudden noises, I had no qualms about setting off a few explosions of my own in celebration of our regained freedom!

WORLD WAR II: STAVANGER FAMILY MEMBERS
by Marilyn Lewis

After the Germans invaded Norway, they set about confiscating as many of the radios that they could. When Uncle Hans heard about this, he was not about to hand over his precious radio, so he hid it in the barn under the hayloft. The German's commandeered the Svendsvoll farm, putting anti-aircraft guns around the perimeter as the farm was in a direct line to the Stavanger airport at Sola. They decided to use the top part of the barn and hayloft for their sleeping quarters, and completely unaware, slept on top of the hidden radio while they stayed at the farm. Uncle Hans worried that his secret cache would be found, but it was not and was retrieved when the Germans left the farm towards the end of the war.

Norway had been invaded on April 9, 1940 by Germany and the planes were constantly flying over the countryside from the airport at Sola. *Oldemor,* great-grandmother Anna Johannesson, a widow, was at home on the farm in Litlaland. She was old and frail and told everyone in the family she was going to bed to die. The family tried in vain to persuade her to go to the farm at Voll, but she was too stubborn. Finally cousin Odd Undem took matters into his own hands. He borrowed a car and drove out to Anna's farm. He and another cousin picked Oldemor out of bed, blankets and all, and put her in the car and drove to Voll. They were able to take some personal items with them. Two days later, a German plane was shot down and crashed in the front yard of Anna's home, burst into flames and burned the house down. Anna remained at Voll until she died in June of 1940.

THOUGH THE MOUNTAINS DEPART:
FUGLESTADS UNDERGROUND

by Swanhild Marie Aalgaard, submitted by JoAn Nellermoe

Fuglestad family members in Norway had been experiencing World War II in far different ways from those of their American relatives. A Norwegian politician, named Vidkun Quisling, betrayed his country and became its puppet ruler, April 9, 1940. Loyal Norwegians immediately began building a resistance movement, known as the "Underground." Torkel Fuglestad and Anna Aarestad's nieces and nephews became involved. They helped sabotage the German rule and aided those fleeing from the clutches of the Gestapo. Before war's end, one hundred five people from the small Bjerkreim community were arrested or had to go into hiding.

Among those in the resistance movement were Torkel and Anna's brother, Thomas's daughter Inga, her husband Jonas Vaule, and five sons and a daughter: Sigurd, Kjell, Tor, Jon, and Alfhild. Attesting to their valor, framed documents hung on the wall of their homes, after the war, as long as the Vaules were alive. Those documents were signed by King Olav, who was Crown Prince during the war; British Prime Minister, Clement Atlee; and General Marshall Montgomery.

The Vaules were part of an early encounter between resisters and the Germans. Two hundred Germans encircled the Geitrams Mountain, on which nineteen members of the Underground were trapped, because a

Norwegian had betrayed them. All nineteen escaped, thanks to the Vaule family. The informer had difficulty sitting down for a time. A shot had grazed his retreating posterior.

For some time the Vaule home was a refuge for members of the Underground, in the Bjerkreim area, as they were hunted by the Germans.

During the months immediately following the German occupation, the Vaules maintained a shortwave broadcasting unit in their attic. By prior arrangement, a British plane had dropped a radio operator, with necessary equipment, on the Vaule farm. This farm provided an ideal location for a spy. It was secluded, yet it commanded a sweeping view of the Norwegian coast from Forsund to Haugesund. Underground spies identified cargoes of specific ships in the Egersund harbor, and that information was secretly relayed to the operator at Vaule. If the ships contained critical war materials, the message was sent to England. Then bombers were sent from England to sink the ships. This was a successful operation for some time. However, the Germans began to realize that vital information was being broadcast from the Bjerkreim area. One night they began closing in on the Vaule home. The Vaules fled.

That frightening night, Jonas Vaule stumbled through the darkness to Svelaodden. There he stripped in order to cross the lake. Just then some Germans drove by.

Jonas cowered under some willows. Then he tied his clothes on his head and swam to safety.

His daughter, Alfhild, crawled under a brush pile, near a road heavily traveled by Germans. She lay there a day and a night. At last, stiff, sore, and hungry, she stealthily ventured back to her home in Svela.

Kjell Vaule clambered up a cliff called Stonjae. At 11:00 p.m. he reached a small shelf near the top of the cliff. As he paused, he realized he could go neither up nor down in the darkness. Water trickling down the cliff collected in a depression in the shelf. Kjell found himself squatting in icy water, no matter how he twisted and turned. At 5:00 a.m. his endurance ran out. Stiffened by cold, he scrabbled down the cliff. "I might as well kill myself in a fall, as to freeze to death in a pool of water," he reasoned. Not even a German cannon trained on the cliff could have kept him shelved. In a warm barn at Svela, he thawed out. Later he was captured, however. Sent to Grini, he remained a prisoner until war's end. He was forcibly trained to be an officer in the German army and was a sergeant for three years.

One bad night, however, was not enough to deter Inga and Jonas from their work in the Resistance Movement. The Germans remained suspicious. September 3, 1944, two men affiliated with the Vaule Underground station, were captured. One of the Vaules' neighbors saw the arrest. Frantically, he biked to the Vaule home. At 1:00 a.m. he aroused the occupants of Vaules' and their neighbor's home. They released their horses and cattle from the barns, then fled. Two hours later the Gestapo found only livestock cropping turnip tops and munching ripened grain hung to dry on the *hesjos.*

Inga and her neighbors fled south toward Vikesaa. As they paused to rest on a mountainside, they realized, looking at Kleppelid, in the valley below, that there was not one house to which they dared go. They stumbled on toward Liknes. Two cars filled with Germans, coming down the road, sent them scurrying behind some rocks. At Oygaard, they crept into a barn loft. Just as they were about to drop off into an exhausted sleep, they were alerted by the sound of approaching voices. A contingent of German soldiers were making a routine search for resisters. One of the soldiers climbed into the hayloft, but his cursory glance did not uncover the fugitives.

As soon as the soldiers left, the fugitives crept out. They struggled on, footsore and bone-tired, over Asheim Mountain. Near Kirkland they stopped to rest on the slop of Stoga Mountain. Inga and her neighbor, Gunhild, decided to make a desperate move. They would return to Vaule for more supplies. Gunhild, who was limping by then, had picked up a stick for support. Inga carried a small sack on her back. So exhausted they could hardly put one foot in front of the other, they inched along, unaware they were being watched.

Two men sat on Stoga Mountain. Looking at the approaching women through his binoculars, one murmured, "I seem to be seeing some witches! Shall I shoot?"

His young companion grabbed the binoculars. "No! It is mother."

The radio operator from Vaule and one of Inga's sons scrambled their way down the mountainside to the women. When the four approached the Vaule home at about 7:30 in the evening, they met a neighbor. Reconnoitering, he had discovered that the Germans had confiscated most of the Vaule property. That which they had not taken, they had dumped into one room of the house. Many thrashed items were long-cherished ones. The Vaules did not dare take a thing. Desperate for sleep, they dropped into the hay in their own barn that night. In the morning they each went their own way.

Inga wandered from place to place, not daring to stay with any friends or relatives for any length of time, lest she endanger them.

The Underground contacted her and determined her movements. First they placed her in a Stavanger hospital as a maternity patient, under an assumed name. Only one doctor and the hospital administrator knew her identity. Dr. Brekke gave her many tests which had to be sent to Bergen for results in order to delay her stay. The admissions director, however, began to make inquiries about the healthy looking patient who was staying so long. Dr. Brekke hastily released her.

She was spirited from house to house. Generally she served as a maid, under various assumed names. In one wealthy home, frequently visited by Germans, she encountered a Nazi whose presence sent her outdoors on a hurried errand. She knew he would recognize her Bjerkreim dialect if he heard her speak. She informed the Underground that she had to be moved quickly.

For three weeks more she was moved from house to house. Finally, along with several other refugees, she was brought to a cottage deep in the forest, near Oslo. There she took charge so effectively that she received special commendation from the chief director of the Underground. A week later, one early morning, a boat picked up the group of refugees, of which Inga was a part, and brought them to Havstensund, Sweden.

Eventually Inga became Refugee No. 64096, at Hedemora, Sweden. By then she knew that Alfhild and Jon were also in Sweden. Of the rest of her family she knew nothing. Brooding about their situation was futile, so she busied herself knitting socks and mittens for Norwegian soldiers.

One May day in 1945, she was, at long last, handed aboard a train bound for Norway. Ironically, she rode the train which carried German prisoners of war on their way home. There were eleven hundred of them—and Inga!

Home at Vaule again, she learned what had happened to the rest of her family. Jonas and Alfhild had fled to a mountain hay shed until morning, that September night. Then they began to cross the Kutjorn Marsh. A German soldier spotted them. Immediately he began shooting at them. They stopped and raised their hands to indicate surrender. He continued to shoot. So they turned to continue their struggle through the marsh, while bullets splashed about them. Alfhild stopped to roll in the mud, in order to make her white dress less conspicuous. The soldier did not pursue them. The next day, assisted by Underground members, they arrived in a fugitive's camp in Sweden.

Jonas and Inga's son Sigurd, was arrested in Oslo just before he would have slipped into Sweden. The Nazis taped his mouth shut to muffle his screams, as they tortured him. For part of their sadistic enjoyment, they removed his shoes and brutalized the soles of his feet. When they tired of tormenting him, they sent him to the prison in Stavanger. He was scheduled for execution by a firing squad, May 13th. May 8, 1945, the Germans capitulated.

Tor Vaule fled to his aunt Selma's home at Berland. From there he managed to get to England. Trained in espionage, he joined a group of saboteurs in Northern Norway until war's end.

Alf Vaule had been captured by the Germans shortly after the occupation of Norway. Sent to a camp in Eikeland he contracted polio. He died within a few days, on May 1, 1944.

Inga's brother, Torkel, managed to retrieve one of the radios which the Germans had confiscated. He kept it in the loft of the Vikesaa schoolhouse, bringing it to his nearby home, only in the evening. Then every evening, neighbors, one by one stole into his home. His living room was generally filled to capacity as the Norwegians listened eagerly to BBC news. This clandestine daily meeting was never discovered by the Germans.

Torkel's son, Torfinn was arrested twice by the Gestapo. The first time he was caught, as he attempted to pick up some weapons that his aunt and uncle Vaule had cached. He and two others were jailed in Stavanger for fourteen days, then released.

One night a month later, he was again picked up. When the Nazis reached Vatnedal, halfway between Fuglestad and Soyland, in Gjesdal, they stopped the car, pulled him out and beat him until he vomited blood. No one heard his screams. They imprisoned him in Akershus Prison, Oslo until war's end. Prison was a grim affair at best, and Akershus under the German regime was even worse.

The war cut deeply into the hearts and lives of Ingeborg Thomasdatter and Sim Sangholt, too.

Their oldest son Karsten, in 1934, was member of the King's Guard. As such he received the king's special commendation.

Later he joined the merchant marines. He had an emergency appendectomy in England. Two days later, he became so violently ill that he was rushed into surgery again. To the doctors' chagrin, they discovered that someone had left a bandage roll in him. He recovered, but not to the satisfaction of the merchant marine officials.

He married and had two children, Atle and Else Margrete.

Being a family man did not squelch his love for the sea, however. In 1940 he was on a freighter, bound for

America. When he heard that his homeland had been overrun by Germany, he fretted, for the first time, because he was at sea. He felt he should be in Norway, fighting the invaders. His freighter was ordered about, but not to England. It was sent to Iran to pick up benzene. He was caught by a seven-month tour of duty.

Once back in England, he hurried to volunteer for espionage. He reveled in his assignments and once remarked, "At last I have found a job which suits me!"

One of his assignments was to head a group of saboteurs who would mine Edoyfjord, near Kristiansund. The mines were to be deposited through a special opening which had been cut out of the side of the ship. A heavy storm sent waves crashing through that special opening. The boat rolled as it edged into Edoyfjord, and some of the mines rolled out of the ship onto the rocks. Incredibly, they were not detonated. By the time the men had finished laying the mines, the storm was so wild that a wave which struck the ship broadside, cracked the whole bottom of the ship. Its engine was knocked out. Frantically, the crew hoisted sails, then all hands bailed water. They were able to land near Kristiansund, but there the ship sank.

Scrambling ashore, they appropriated a rowboat and headed farther down the coast. On the south shore of Romsdalsfjorden, they managed to hire a driver willing to take them to a point from which they might return to England. The only road, however, ran right through a Nazi camp. At one point the road was so narrow that the driver had to stop in order to permit an oncoming car to pass. The other car stopped. Under their oilskins all five men were wearing English uniforms. Holding their breath, they sat with fingers on cocked revolver triggers, as the Germans walked toward them. Incredibly, the soldiers only glanced at them, then motioned the driver on. As they began to breathe again, they looked at one another in wonder.

The next day the Germans realized whom they had failed to capture. Then they instigated a house-by-house search. The soldiers had come to the house next to the one in which Karsten and his men were hiding, before the saboteurs knew what was happening. They bolted for the shore. There they confiscated a motorboat. They made the Shetland Island the next day. Later they heard that their bold venture had resulted in two German ships having been blown up.

November 10, 1941, Karsten and his men made another run to Norway to deliver weapons and ammunition. Returning, they were caught by a hurricane. Something on the deck broke loose, threatening other fixtures. Karsten struggled out on the deck to secure the object. Just then the vessel was struck broadside by an enormous wave. When the craft righted itself, Karsten was gone.

Caught by the German blockade, Karsten's wife and children had to remain in Northern Norway. Not until four years later did they learn of Karsten's death. His wife Anna was prostrated. His son Atle proudly received the Norwegian Medal of Honor posthumously awarded Karsten. Later he also went to sea.

Ingeborg and Simon Sangolt's daughter Aslaug (Mrs. Alf Gundersen) was living in Bergen, in 1944, when a German munitions ship exploded in port, leveling much of the city. Aslaug's house was destroyed, but she and her children survived. When the worst was over, she went out to look at the demolished city. Then she knew she had to leave at once.

She moved home to Sangholt. There she made the house a shelter for fugitives fleeing to England. Among them was her cousin Tor Vaule. At one time she was trying feed fifteen people under a tight rationing system. Only the fact that people from the Bjerkreim area kept sending her ration cards saved the situation.

In 1940 Ingeborg and Simon Sangolt's son, Tomas, with thirteen other men crowded into a boat, were bound for the Shetland Island. Betrayed by an informer, their craft was gunned down. All aboard were lost.

Kjellaug Sangholt worked for her aunt Selma Gaasland, at Berland, in Bjerkreim. She was there when the Gaaslands had to flee. She alone remained on the farm. The Gestapo questioned her several times, but, ever capricious, they did not try to harm her.

Ivar Thomasson Fuglestad was a contact man for the Underground. He transported fugitives to his sister Selma Gaasland's farm. He also took great risks as he secured weapons and passports to Sweden, for the fugitives, in Stavanger. Someone betrayed him. Soldiers held his family at bay with a machine gun, while others searched the Fuglestad house until they found him.

175

He was jailed in Egensveien, in Stavanger. There he was tortured and interrogated for two weeks. But when the Gestapo could not thus discover his vital role in the Underground, they released him in obvious disgust.

Selma and Torleif Gaasland provided a fugitive center. They build a cleverly concealed hut, deep in the woods. Some foolhardy refugees brought weapons which they insisted on using in target practice. The shots resounding through the countryside did not soothe their host and hostess's nerves.

The Gaaslands were caught in a web of constant tension. October 17, 1944, for instance, the Gestapo arrested a man who knew the details of the activities at Berland. Selma and Torleif fled for a few days.

They had just returned to Berland when the Germans confiscated all automobiles and arrested people whether they had any connection with the Resistance Movement or not. They forced the sheriff to guide them to Berland. He was to lead them to the fugitives' hideout in the woods. This he could not do, since he had no idea of its location.

Selma and her niece Kjellaug Sangholt were caught in the house and guarded there. One of the guards was a Norwegian traitor. Selma begged him for permission to go the barn to feed the horses. Once there, she slipped off her wooden shoes. Carrying them, she raced up the hillside, in full view of the soldiers in the house. Miraculously, they did not see her. On through the woods she sped, to the fugitives' hut. Warned, the fugitives fled farther into the forest to await darkness. Then they regrouped to decide how to scatter to safety.

Selma and oldest son Trygve, spent about a week in a shelter under a large rock at the boundary between Fuglestad and Nedrebo. Then they ventured back to Berland, determined to face whatever happened.

In the meantime Torleif had hurried south to hide in Heskestad. Three weeks before Christmas he also returned to Berland. Jonas Vaule and his son, Sigurd, arrived a few days later. Christmas Eve at Berland was not a joyful occasion as no food remained in the house. Selma went to borrow flour and butter from neighbors, but no one dared to help her. She then went all the way to her brother Trygve's flour mill in Vikesaa. The three men at Berland, in the meantime, butchered a pig.

The Germans, living in the chapel in Vikesaa, had patrols scouring the countryside for members of the Underground, and for those who dared to hide these resisters. Even though they had cut the telephone line to Berland, someone always managed to warn the Gaaslands when the Germans were headed for Berland. When they realized their presence was being betrayed, the Germans changed their route.

One day they stole quietly through the Berland woods. Torleif, accompanied by his two dogs, had gone there to chop wood. Before he began his work, he stopped to pat the dogs. As he did, he spotted a soldier hiding behind some bushes. He beat a stealthy retreat. To his consternation, he saw Trygve carrying water from a hole cut in the lake ice, to the cattle in the barn. Torleif quickly ran into the house to warn Jonas and Sigrud. The three men then sprinted across the year to an outdoor toilet. There they crawled through a trap door into a tunnel which led to a secret compartment under the hay in the barn.

One of the soldiers, watching from the other side of the farm, saw Torleif and his two dogs dash across the ice to the house. He rushed into the farmyard moments after the three fellows had squeezed into their hiding place.

Speaking broken Norwegian, he approached Trygve. "The man with the two dogs?" he asked, as he pointed to the frozen lake.

"It was I," Trygve answered.

"*Two* men and two dogs?" The German was becoming impatient.

Fourteen-year-old Kaare just then approached, carrying a pail of water in each hand.

"It was I!"

The exasperated German fired a salvo into the frozen ground, directly in front of Trygve's feet. One of the bullets ricocheted through the second story of the house.

The other soldier, attracted by the shots, came running from his hiding place in the woods. Frustrated though they were, they had to leave, in the face of the continuing protestations of the two boys.

Selma, watching through a kitchen window, with pounding heart, prayed fervently. Then she stopped to wonder why they neither questioned nor arrested her. As she thought about it, she suspected they might want to leave her as a lure, to catch fugitives.

The fact that they could not prove that resisters were being hidden at Berland so enraged the Germans that they announced that *anyone* going to Berland after dark would be shot.

They restored phone service to Berland, then planted a man in the telephone exchange. The Norwegians were still able to intercept messages given to the Germans, as to when there were fugitives at Berland, as well as to know when Torleif and Trygve might be caught. Always the Gaaslands were warned in time. One evening Selma's brother, Georg, risked his life to warn them. As a precaution he loaded his sled with wood and rode homeward, singing all the way. Thereby he avoided being shot, as the Germans had threatened.

Trygve and Torleif, who had fled in response to that warning, wearied of flight. Three weeks later they returned to Berland. They built another shelter in a thick stand of evergreens for Torleif. They made a trapdoor under the kitchen linoleum and found space just large enough for Trygve, under the house. The soldiers, suspicious of just such a hiding place, tried hard to find it, yet, strangely, they never succeeded.

The Gaaslands were familiar with the Scriptures and were often reminded of the Psalmist's words, "Many are the afflictions of the righteous, but the Lord delivereth him out of them all." (Psalms 34:19) Once, after a raid, they noticed the twentieth verse, "He kept all his bones; not one of them is broken." They remembered how Torleif had had time only to squirm under hay in the barn loft. The searching soldier had grabbed a pitchfork with which he prodded the hay all around Torleif, yet he missed him and left him unscathed.

A Norwegian traitor was responsible for the cat and mouse games at Berland. Eventually he was identified, but only after he had created many dangerous situations for the Gaaslands. Although the Germans kept pouncing until war's end, they never caught Torleif, Trygve, or the fugitives who came and went at Berland.

War's end found Norway depleted of material goods. Members of the various Fuglestad families were in need of clothes, and the American Fuglestads responded out of their relative plenty, by sending packages of clothing and other supplies. Out of that need came a special bond between the family members.

Finally, after war's end, the Fuglestads, American and Norwegian alike, began, day by day, piece by piece, to put their disrupted lives together again.

NORWEGIAN WORLD WAR II ROOTS
IN THE STAVANGER AREA
by Kirk Beiningen

I was born in 1937, so my memories of World War 2 are limited to my childhood experiences while living in Steilacoom, Walla Walla and Seattle, Washington.

The only first-hand knowledge I have of WW 2 in Norway came from relatives I met during my visits to the south-west coastal island of Karmøy and nearby Stavanger. In conversations with Daniel Torkelsen in 1962 and his son Jarl in 1998, I learned a little about the occupation in that area by German armed forces. The house where my father's father was born lies just east of Skudeneshavn, at a place called Auste. Between the town and Auste lies the community of Beiningen, where my grandfather lived before emigrating to America. Beiningen was inhabited by ships' pilots, who guided ocean-going vessels coming from the North Sea into Skudenesfjorden, Karmsundet, and Boknafjorden. The shoreline south of Beiningen held a lighthouse, a few huts, and a tower used by the ships' pilots to sight incoming ships.

This southern tip of the island of Karmøy was militarily important to the Germans. It was an obvious place to set up fortifications, artillery and observation platforms, and fortified bunkers so as to guard the shoreline. A search light and gun emplacements were installed at the lighthouse at Beiningen. Remnants are still visible today. German troops were stationed in Beiningen

181

to man their installations. The house at Auste was commandeered as a residence for German officers. Near the end of the war one of the officers got drunk and fired his pistol in the house. One of the rounds struck a grandfather clock at about 5 o'clock. One could have said that he was killing time until the end of the hostilities.

My other wartime experience had to do with Norwegian-Americans in this country. My folks and I lived in Steilacoom, situated between Tacoma and Fort Lewis, Washington. I was in the first grade at Steilacoom Grade School in 1942. Across the street from my school lived a family with the last name of Grondahl. They had a son in the US Army Air Corps, stationed at nearby McChord Air Base. One day, as Bill was returning from a training flight, he decided to say hello to his folks by flying close to the ground as he flew over Steilacoom. He scared the whole town. My grandfather was a volunteer at an aircraft observation tower near our house, and thought that we were under attack. Needless to say that event made an impression on everyone in Steilacoom that day.

Twenty-one years later I was taking a Norwegian language class at the University of Washington. I asked an attractive classmate out for a coffee date. She introduced herself as Molly Grondahl. I told her about my scary childhood experience getting buzzed by an airplane. She said that the pilot was her cousin, Bill Grondahl.

Molly and I have visited Norway several times. We came to appreciate what the Norwegians there experienced during the war.

Chapter 4: Northern Norway

MEMORIES FROM VOLDSMINDE:
GERMANS ON SKIS
by Egil Furunes

(This is a translation from Norwegian accomplished by using the Google translator. The results from that were less than satisfactory. I have attempted to correct all the problems. The resulting document is, however, not perfect. My goal was to make it readable in English and, above all, to maintain the meaning that the original writer wanted to convey. Please read with forgiving eyes.

Bjorn Heglie, 10 January, 2012

Watching the German soldiers who were learning to ski was some of the most fun we could experience. It was for us a pleasant sight, the completely helpless trying to learn the elementary art of skiing. In a helpless and wide track they staggered off. On flat ground it went fairly well until the skis started to separate and they performed the wide splits or they leaned too far backwards and tumbled to the ground at their backs. Then the fun really began. Some remained deadlocked with poles under them, while others managed to merge skis and falling on their backs on top of their skis. It was priceless comedy to regard their helpless attempts to get up. Some who had managed to get into a sitting position tried time and again to rise by using the poles. The result was the same each time, skis went ahead and German backwards. After a fierce battle in unsuccessful attempts to stand up, snowmen were helped or they took their skis off. Down the slopes they went without regard for their lives. Everything from the simplest falls to nasty somersaults and harsh meetings with trees and bushes that lined the slopes. They persevered and did not give up, even though they understood that their hardships were a great pleasure for us.

Especially fun it was when they practiced in full equipment with backpack and carbine crossed in from of chest. Then both the falls and the subsequent difficulty getting up was even more fun to watch. Practice makes perfect, it says, and if this did not apply to everyone, they managed it at last to master the skis and stand down the slopes in their own way. It was a tradition that our family was skiing every Sunday from the first snow to the last vestiges disappeared after Easter. My first pair of skis I got for Christmas that year I turned two years old, and from then on I was participating regularly on trips. At first I was a bit clumsy between mother and father, but mostly I sat on top of my father's backpack. Later I became more skilled and got up the hills, often benefited either by a rope father had attached to his backpack or I hung on one of his poles. That is how I learned early to ski downhill and there was never any ground that was too difficult or steep, on the contrary, the faster the better. This story is necessary to introduce the following event: It was a brilliant ski Sunday, sun from a cloudless sky and we should take a trip on Grønnlia and Skistua. As usual, the trip started from the top of Steinberget, to make the most of the day we were always early. As a rule, we were on our way already around eight or half past eight.

The ski condition was good, so the trip to Grønnlia went "like clockwork," and after a picnic on a sunny hillside, with coffee and what a packed lunch had to offer, the trip to Skistua was a breeze. After a brief stop there, and a refusal to get a run down Rustad Renna, because we were to go through Lian, and so it was useless to discuss with father. From experience I knew to push further would not lead to anything good. Quite miffed, labored I therefore against Skistumyra and trail down to Lian, while parents got a little way behind. As I said, I had good glide on skis and enjoyed slow running on the slack slope down to the marsh. In front of me and in the same vein, I discovered a German ski patrol in full gear. Wearing their white ski clothes with the big sack on his back and the mauser across the chest. It would have been an impressive sight if skiing proficiency had been in harmony with their looks. But seven to eight Germans in full gear was scary enough that no one demanded free tracks by shouting the usual "track"! It was fast enough that the Germans, unsteady as they were, had a wide track and tried to brake with a ski on each side of the track. From behind I came, still a bit grumpy and with much better speed, I had no intention to slow down by changing tracks. "Track"! I cried as loud as I could, but no reaction, however, as I rapidly approached the Germans. Well huddled and right on skis, I heard mother cry something, but too late. Between the legs of the straddling German I sped like a bullet, and one after the other was "run through." There were shouts and screams behind me where they were falling. It was fully chaos when the two of them fell on their butt and ran into each other. Some of them were fighting mad as I heard their cries and what I later was told by others. I got a real scolding and told never to repeat that again.

My parents, who with fright had to see what their little darling had done, stayed close to me as we hurried on way toward Lian. The consequences of stopping could be serious. Thus they preferred not to make it more exciting than it all was. On the way down we passed another small ski patrol, but at a distance. There was no stop at Lian this time, but right down town and home. All in all it had been a successful tour, although with a somewhat unexpected excitement. However, I am one of the few who have managed to foil a whole team of Germans without using bullets and gunpowder.

NARVIK AND NORTHERN NORWAY
by Birgit Hanssen and Astri Grieg Fry

I was born in March, 1928, in the Ofotenfjord, close to Narvik and the Ballangen area in Northern Norway.

Before the war, I had a happy childhood. The youngest of four siblings, I was close to my mother, and I enjoyed activities such as being a girl scout and delivering newspapers.

At the onset of World War II, I was a sixth grade twelve-year-old. The high school was a new building, but the Germans confiscated it and I attended high school in an old school building. The main teacher there was an army major who fought during the war. When he was taken prisoner, his wife took his place as a teacher, and their oldest son helped out.

In those days ownership was in the hands of a few. A capitalist might own an island or a factory. In our case, this applied to the Bjørkaasen mines. Executives were the privileged class with special homes and stores. People speaking in many different dialects came from all over Norway to work there, but there were numerous accidents and fatalities. Conditions in those deep mines were such that many miners died young, leading to the whole operation being shut down after the war, in 1946. My dad owned a grocery store. Often the miners would buy from him on credit, and I would be sent to the mine owner's office to collect from the miners' next wages. One day during 1940, when my dad was taking a nap at lunchtime, smoke was seen coming from the store. It was on fire. My family salvaged what it could as everything was in such short supply during this time. Then we moved to my grandparents' farm a little farther south of Narvik close to the ocean and remained there for about a year.

Other family occupations were, for example, my oldest sister working as a switchboard operator which was a common job for girls in that time and place. One aunt was a nurse and one uncle had been a carpenter, but after joining the military, was taken prisoner. My grandfather expressed his disapproval of the Germans during the war by shaking his cane as their planes flew overhead—then fell down and died.

The Germans were anxious to take control of Narvik because of access to iron ore supplies from Sweden. This led to intense naval battles in Narvik during the first two months of the war (as of early April 1940), with fighting on the fjord between British and German warships. One smaller British warship in particular was affected by both German torpedoes and adverse tides. The injured crew from the damaged British ship took refuge in local houses, and the community center, Folkets Hus, supplied them with clothing and food. Funeral services were held for the British who were killed in the naval battles, and they were buried in the local graveyard. This included a funeral for a high-ranking British officer, and during his service, my dad wept. As a result of these naval battles, live ammunition ended up on the rocky mountainside shores. Some of this was in the form of unexploded torpedoes. Concealed by the snow at first, once it melted by mid-May or so, the residents had to be on guard as to what sort of debris they handled and picked up. Other residents had begun evacuating when the fighting began.

At one point there was a lighter side to this situation. A French allied force had deposited some supplies in our area. The residents were hoping to discover some good French wine, but instead came across spices for French cooking. However, everyone accepted whatever was available and secreted it from the Germans amongst potato field greenery.

During my high school years, there were Russian soldiers imprisoned in a nearby camp. The Germans would march the Russian prisoners to some work project and we saw them pass by in the extreme cold. We looked for anything we could give these Russians, and if we had any money, we threw them the coins which they picked up. At the end of the war when it was time for these soldiers to return home, they cried—but these were not tears of joy. Rumor had it that they might be shot upon their return home. Firstly for the shame of having been taken prisoner by the Germans and secondly suspected of possible collaboration with the enemy—in other words, considered traitors.

The Germans began retreating from Northern Norway by the fall of 1944, in the face of the advancing Russian forces. As they retreated, they burned churches, schools, homes—anything and everything that would go up in flames—only a very few buildings were spared. Many people evacuated southward or to Sweden. Others took refuge in caves in the Arctic wilderness during that grim winter of 1944-45.

MY CHILDHOOD IN ANKENES DURING WW II
by Petter Moe

At the onset of World War II, I, Petter, was six. I lived with my parents, my two older brothers and my older sister in Ankenes (Ankenesstrand), across-fjord from Narvik in Northern Norway.

On the morning of the German invasion on April 9, 1940, the shaking of my small bed awoke me. Looking out the window, only flashes from cannon fire could be seen through the driving snow. That week my parents were in Harstad, attending the funeral of my mother's brother Størker Størkersen, a noted Polar explorer. My mother was from a farm outside of Harstad called Skuven, one of eleven surviving children. During their absence, my parents had hired a nanny to be in charge of the household. She and her young child stayed with us until we got to Tysfjord.

Getting news that we had to evacuate, my sister dressed me as well as herself, and I am sure my brothers as well, as there were very cold conditions at the time. I was dressed in layers upon layers of clothing until a little kid like me could hardly move. Once I was packed into all my layers, my sister and I ventured forth into the freezing cold to buy food we could take with us when we were evacuated. Suitcases were packed and we walked to the assembly place in the town square of Ankenes where we were put on the first available car and driven off, nanny and all. After stopping later at a school, my family got out as this was our destination. The car and the others we had

191

been with drove off without us. This was the last we saw of our luggage on top of the car as someone forgot to unload our precious and only possessions. My brothers were able to replenish our food supplies, but my sister, the nanny and I were separated from my brothers. After that I did not see them until later in Harstad. We did not know what was going to happen or how long we were going to be there. While waiting at the evacuation center at the school, I remember waking up at one point and seeing that one child's thirst made him drink black ink from a school desk's inkwell while his mother became hysterical.

The next day we were brought by ferry to the ferry landing at Virak where we stayed overnight. In the morning, again I was awakened by cannon fire. I could not reach up to the window to see out until I found a crate to stand on. There was a sea-battle going on outside in the fjord. The ships had different camouflage colors. It was explained later that the ships were British and German. I watched two of the ships being sunk. Once they were hit, the rear of the ships lifted up in the air and they went straight down, bow first. After they sank, another British ship circled around to pick up survivors floating in the water. I stood watching the battle until my sister found me and made me climb down off my crate. I did not know it at the time, but metal shrapnel was flying all the way up to the house where we were staying, and it was extremely dangerous to be standing by a fjord-facing window.

On the third day, we were evacuated to Skjomen, staying with some people there for several weeks. After the war was over, my parents became good friends with them, spending summers together visiting, picking berries and sharing farm goods. After that, my sister and I, as well as our nanny, were moved on to the Kiel family at Tysfjord. During this time my sister became my surrogate mother. The rest of my family was scattered and we did not know where they all were. In my mind, she was the only one I had left in the world. This formed a lasting and unbreakable bond between us.

Another memory from this time of chaos is attending a meeting of a religious sect that my sister and a friend of hers wanted to go to in Tysfjord. My sister was trying to get on with her life as though nothing had happened, and that meant going to church without her baby brother. I, on the other hand, was terrified at the prospect of being left behind. So I screamed at the top of my lungs and banged on the window until I was included. Once we got to the church, I started to laugh hysterically when I heard the congregation humming mantras during the meeting. My sister had to tuck my head under her jacket to muffle my mirth. I had never been in a group like this and was completely unprepared for this type of religious observance and didn't know what to make of it at all, being only six years old.

In Tysfjord, the nanny left with her child to rejoin her husband, leaving me alone with my sister. Meanwhile my brothers had ended up in Harstad (where my mother and father were staying), after at first volunteering with the Allied forces in Bjerkvik. The Allied forces consisted of

Norwegian, British and French troops, plus French Legionnaires, Polish and Czechoslovakian free forces. As they were only fifteen and seventeen at the time, my brothers were too young to actually join the forces. However, they spent their time carrying munitions, running errands and assisting as best they could.

When I next saw my parents, I barely recognized them—four months being how long it took for them to trace us and pick us up by boat. Until then, while we knew where they were, they had known nothing of our whereabouts until we were traced.

Immediately before the invasion, Norwegian waters leading into Narvik had been mined by the British to block the Germans' control of the pig iron supply from Sweden, which was a vital material for high quality steel production of tanks, cannons and warships. Narvik, with its ice-free fjord, was a principal harbor for international ships as the Baltic ports were iced in over the winter time. However, Hitler used the British mining of Norwegian waters as one of his pretexts for invading Norway. At the onset of the war, the Germans patrolled the Narvik fjords with submarines at the mouth of the fjords, and with frigates and destroyers farther in. The British arrived with a battleship, several frigates and destroyers and sank numerous German warships. In the crossfire, the Norwegian battleships *Eidsvold* and *Norge* went down. These dated from the early part of the century and were our only battleships on site. The Narvik naval battles were intense at the beginning of the war.

Throughout the war, a tremendous amount of Swedish pig iron passed through Narvik harbor annually. However, Narvik's significance faded as German forces concentrated their efforts on Great Britain and France. The Allied forces moved out to support the British and French forces after the Battle of Dunkirk, leaving Narvik and the population in Northern Norway to the mercy of the Germans. As a result, Norwegian forces capitulated.

Meanwhile, on the more personal level, the sheriff of Ankenes was responsible for finding out where my family was and notified my parents. When my parents found out where we were, they sent friends to Tysfjord to pick us up by fishing boat. This boat was strafed by a German airplane, and the friends had to make it to shore and run for cover. No one was hurt, and the boat was not touched by bullets. Soon after, the British were patrolling the fjord, so our friends tried again to make it from Harstad to Tysfjord to pick us up. During this trip the ferry passed by an English battleship in the fjord. I remember the English sailors tossing coins down to us, but the deck of the ferry was a grating so the coins went right through the grating and I did not catch a single one, even though I really wanted those coins.

My sister and I were reunited with our parents in Harstad. Our brothers had already been united with our parents, and they were all waiting on the beach for us. There still were heavy battles going on in Narvik. The German forces were bombarding the city. Once the hostilities were over and the German forces were occupying Narvik, it became safe to travel by sea again. My family and I took a small passenger boat from Harstad to Narvik some time later. The captain, Kaptein Nyborg, was the man who owned the house we lived in, and he invited me in to the captain's cabin for a friendly chat. I remember that this was a great honor.

Petter, center, with siblings

After our return to Narvik following the evacuation, we heard that 33 ships had sunk in the Narvik harbor. For a while, multiple ship smokestacks and masts were on view sticking up out of the water. These were ultimately leveled by dynamite to clear the way for the regular shipping traffic that started to build up.

After these initial battles, somehow life had to go on. During the evacuation, my brothers, sister and I had lost our suitcases filled with clothing, food, and personal items, last seen driving away on top of the evacuation car. When we returned home, we discovered that a number of our personal possessions also had disappeared from our home which had been looted. Silverware, picture frames, china— if it could be carried away, it was gone. However, my parents found some of our things outside on the trails as they had been left there by the looters.

Before the war, my father had worked in sheet metal construction. However, now with normal business being at a standstill, he scaled back to producing everyday items such as teakettles and pails which my mother traded for cheese and butter. In addition to running the farm, my mother picked lingonberries to make into jam. Then these food treasures were sent to relatives in towns where food was even scarcer. At this time, everything was rationed: flour, vegetables, butter, eggs, alcohol. Even if you could buy it from the store, supplies were limited by the Germans. Because of my mother's generosity towards our relatives in other towns, we sometimes felt shortchanged at home, but that was our mother and father's decision. They were the workers and we kids, we were just helpers. We still were better off than many others.

Besides sharing food, we shared our home. During the evacuation during the winter of 1944-45, I often woke up in the morning, stepping over new combinations of visiting relatives and their friends who had been burned out of their homes by the German forces in Finnmark. "If there is room in your heart, there is room in your house," said my mother. In addition to being a refuge for friends and relatives who then traveled on to other places, we also had a family living upstairs. They shared daily life with us as a family due to the loss of their home which had been burnt down during the hostilities.

At our local school, my godfather was the headmaster and my godmother was my teacher. This sometimes made it difficult for a little kid who wanted some elbow room. I never got away with anything. Whenever I complained to my mother that Miss Markussen was much stricter with me than with the other boys, she always said, "Miss Markussen is your godmother, so she must do the right thing for you. Give me a break."

There were six classrooms and the teacher's lounge in our school house, but when the Germans took over the schoolhouse, classes were temporarily held in private homes until we were brought back to our school. The Germans also requisitioned rooms in private houses including in ours. They used one of our living rooms where secretaries and a few junior officers and other functionaries were housed at various times. There was, however, minimal contact between us as this parlor had its own private entrance. Our parents told us never to talk to the Germans. We never did.

Many times I saw two soldiers at our house, in Austrian uniform with an edelweiss pin on their lapels, overseeing Yugoslavian or Russian prisoners delivering supplies to the parlor staff. These Austrian soldiers hated being part of the Germany army, and perhaps that is why they looked away as my mother fed the prisoners salted herring and other things like bread, butter and marmalade. I stared as they devoured the fish, the skin, the bones, leaving only the tails uneaten. My mother then wrapped up extra fish for them in newspaper, which they stuffed into their coat pockets as they left. Sharing was part of our life.

Several miles from our home were two concentration camps where the prisoners worked on road construction. We occasionally put food in the quarry so they could find it. They showed their appreciation in a surprising way. Having somehow retained their knives, they whittled and carved wooden toys for us. One toy was a carved, wooden bird. It was so realistically and cleverly carved that the wings had layered feathers. As kids, we were never allowed too close to the prisoners as they were supervised by soldiers and sometimes by "Waffen-SS."

In the summer we played soccer at the local field, not far from the harbor where the German state yacht *Grille* was moored. The *Grille* was used as a minelayer earlier in the war, but was moored in Narvik from 1942 until the end of the war. This was the official yacht at the personal disposal of Hitler; and used as a command center for the

Arctic U-boats. German state dignitaries, generals and admirals also used the ship for recreational purposes. The Germans had also commandeered the Norwegian cruise ship *Stella Polaris* for their recreational use, taking full advantage of its luxurious amenities. So while kicking the soccer ball and running back and forth, from Hitler's yacht we would hear a sailor blowing a whistle for all he was worth whenever any dignitary boarded or disembarked this vessel. As we heard his extended tones over the water, we thought he surely must be turning blue from lack of air. Both *Grille* and *Stella Polaris* had a U-boat net around the ship, helping to prevent divers from approaching. One day, my neighbors Anton Millejord and Bertil Frederiksen went out fishing in the harbor as they did all the time. On this particular day, they were outside the net, but close to *Stella Polaris*. A nervous German guard on the ship fired at them, killing Bertil immediately. Anton brought Bertil to shore where friends came running to take care of the body. Within an hour after this horrific incident, Anton returned to fish at that same place, making it clear to us and to the Germans that it was his territory. No further shots were ever fired at him. I just loved Anton and would often spend time sitting and helping him to mend his fishing nets. He never spoke much, but it was a great honor to sit beside him and work.

In winter we cross-country skied and often saw German soldiers holding maneuvers. They fired with wooden bullets which disintegrated after they were fired. The result was that we, having wandered a little too close, often had wooden slivers to pick out of our clothing. None of my friends were seriously hurt by this.

So many memories remembered and some forgotten!

In our boathouse by the beach, a Ford car was hidden by a neighbor who since had fled to Sweden and established a business there. My friends and I often played in the car. I had fun taking on the role of "commander" of it, telling my friends what to do as we played around. I played in this car from the age seven until I was twelve. I think it was a light blue 4-door 1932-ish sedan. After the war was over, my neighbor then came back temporarily. He reclaimed the car and went back to his business in Sweden. The car was never discovered by the Germans.

My brothers, on the other hand, being considerably older than me, collected weapons they came across—rifles, machine guns, bayonets, ammunition—anything they could get their hands on, mostly left behind by fallen soldiers. Many of these were buried in the woods and other places on our property, simply buried wherever they fell, remaining there until they were exhumed and put in special graveyards. My brothers hid their stash of weapons in our big tool shed. Discovery of this would probably have meant deportation for my father and brothers or worse.

One neighbor kept his illegal radio in a tea kettle on the stove. If the Germans found an illegal radio, the consequences could be dire. So their plan was that if they ever faced a German *razzia*, they could simply pour boiling water into the kettle and put it on the stove to steep. No one thought the Germans would search a boiling kettle for contraband! Another of my friend's neighbors had been working on his house and run out of plywood. So he sneaked over to the concentration camp when that was being built and helped himself to some of the German's plywood, but was caught and sent to Buchenwald, never to return. We learned to keep our mouths shut and never to snitch.

One day when my mother was expecting guests at lunchtime, a German lieutenant accompanied by a few soldiers, the so-called *razzia,* came to search our house for anything incriminating. My mother ordered the lieutenant to stop the search and, surprisingly, he did after which he and his fellow soldiers left. That same evening my father, now learning of this stash for the first time, along with my brothers removed their hidden booty and deposited it into the deep, dark waters of the harbor. The bayonets and soldiers helmets were stashed away from the house. After the war, whatever remained of surplus "ammo" became entertaining fireworks for kids. This was much to the alarm of the parents, who feared we could be hurt by the shrapnel falling down as we exploded these ordnances.

After the war we housed a Norwegian officer and his family, his wife and one child. They requisitioned a room, the same room that the Germans had during the war. His responsibility was to map military camps, storage facilities and concentration camps. I was lucky to be invited on his tours, driving in a Citroen car. Big stuff for a twelve year old kid right after the war! I got a glimpse of military camps and inspected armaments, including our so-called "Hitler cannon" at Trondnes that controlled the entrance to Ofotfjorden. Also I was included when visiting the prison camps. Not a good sight. Some of my friends were not aware of my excursions with Captain Swendsen, later to become a General of the Norwegian army, as did his son Helge later on. As an adult, I later visited and stayed with them in Oslo several times.

Petter astride a "Hitler cannon"

When the war finally drew to its end, Germans soldiers began retreating from Finnmark and then southward, burning the area to the ground. The "scorched earth" policy left thousands of civilians homeless and destitute in a harsh winter climate. In many places, only the churches were left standing, all other buildings were burned down, and people fled to the woods to hide. In retreat, the

Germans removed military hardware wherever they could so that it wouldn't fall into Russian hands. (The Finns, fighting the Russians, had allied themselves with the Germans.) In retreating from the north, the Germans flooded into Narvik and Ankenes, which were truly bottlenecks, with their equipment. On top of that, there was a flood of refugees coming south, some of them staying with us. Our home was always open to relatives and their friends.

Once Germany had surrendered, those prisoners who had not been killed in any of the camps executions were released, now celebrating and walking freely on the streets. To our great surprise, some of them were men in the Russian uniforms of admirals and generals, and other important prisoners. We always wondered how they had acquired these new uniforms so soon. I never found out, but I suspect they received their uniforms through Sweden, which was close by. Many of these former prisoners of war were returned to Murmansk on board the *Stella Polaris*, which had been released to the Norwegian Ministry of War Transport in 1945.

For some, however, the rejoicing was short-lived. Rumors were that when the Russian prisoners returned to their homeland after their extended internment in the West, they represented a threat to the ideals of Communism. After all they witnessed modern conveniences such as electricity, well-constructed houses with wooden floors rather than dirt ones, and the latest models of kitchen stoves. Rumor had it that many of them were isolated, then sent straight on to Siberian labor camps or gulags by Stalin, never allowed the opportunity to tell of their exposure to any western standard of living.

Even though I was a young boy during World War II, my experiences growing up in wartime have left a lifelong mark. On the difficult side: a great sadness over the destruction and devastating effects of war, of the many thousands who died needlessly on all sides, so many of them young. On the lighter side: learning responsibility from the early age of eight, starting with farm chores at first, then going on to work at lumberyards and pig iron facilities and the railroad. I became self-supporting early, including funding my own education with the money I made and saved as a high school kid working during the summer months. This instilled in me the ability to make decisions with confidence, to think clearly, and to place a high value on the ties of family and friendships. Perhaps this is what encouraged me to explore other parts of Europe and settle down in Portland after securing a job here. I knew that I had family in the Portland area, but did not know all of them before I came here. Upon my arrival, many years ago, I met many family members who were already residing in Portland and Seattle, some thirty-forty of them. Naturally, many were members of Sons of Norway's Grieg Lodge including my aunt Karen Størkersen, who was a founder of The Daughters of Norway.

I felt I had found a new home.

BODØ: COME HELL OR HIGH WATER

by Helga Joyce and Astri Grieg Fry

"ROW!"

And my grandfather and uncle pulled on the oars with all their might and main—literally through hell and high water—while navigating Saltstrømmen (later renamed Saltstraumen). This is the world's strongest and most notorious maelstrom that swirls just to the southeast of Bodø in Northern Norway.

What was I, Helga Haugen, to make of this? I was ten when Norway became occupied by the German forces, and life, as we had known it thus far, changed drastically. There we were on a night in late May, 1940—besides our two oarsmen, five more of us in the family were crammed into a small rowboat. We heard cannon fire from nearby Bodø. At the same time we desperately wanted to avoid being sucked into the maelstrom whirlpools as we evacuated to relative safety across-fjord.

This was only the beginning of our several migrations. Another time we fled to isolated Kodvaag, staying for months with complete strangers who had been pressured to take in refugees. Other evacuations went inland. Up in the hills we constructed camouflage using birch limbs due to planes flying in at close range, shooting at anything that moved, be it people or livestock. Once, outside not far from our house with my toddler brother, we heard a plane coming in at low altitude. As I threw myself over his smaller body, looking up I actually could see the pilot. This was a close encounter affording us no cover, although the pilot ignored us that time, flying onward and out of sight.

Prior to the war we had known a peaceful lifestyle in a rural setting within sight of Bodø to the west of us. Although we had to cross the fjord by rowboat just to get to a store of any kind, at least normally we could time our crossings according to favorable nautical conditions. My grandfather and other family members were *Lofotkarer*, those hardy men who fished the cod runs in their small vessels—in the dead of our Arctic winters. After the fish were netted, they were cleaned, split, salted and hung to dry on massive racks. Once I was old enough, I was able to help out with this work by summertime. (Oddly enough, the Germans did not interfere with our fishing livelihood, which was fortunate. We were poor enough as it was.)

Unlike the fishermen in the family, my stepfather was a miner in faraway Spitsbergen, Svalbard. As early as 1939, he had left for military training in Scotland. He then returned to Spitsbergen to help defend it against any outside aggressors. However, Spitsbergen was soon overrun in 1940 by the Germans, taking control of the coal mines there. Dad was among those taken prisoner and spent the entire five years of the war in German camps: first a prison camp near the Polish border, followed by Luckenwalde (a camp c. 50 km south of Berlin). When he returned after the war, not only had he physically been reduced to skin and bone—his personality likewise had changed. Had he been of a reserved nature before the war, he was much more so in its aftermath. He was most reluctant to talk about his wartime experience.

During the war, my mother waged her own battle, namely to find out what had happened to her husband and whether or not he was dead or alive. She appealed to the nearest German Headquarters for information as well as to the Red Cross. Only after several years did she learn of his imprisonment in Germany and was allowed to send him some letters, albeit censured. She was not permitted to send him anything else—not that we had any goods at our disposal to speak of!

My mother had an apartment near Bodø, but living there was constantly disrupted for us during the war. There were multiple forced evacuations. When forced to leave Bodø, we often stayed instead at my grandparents' farm. Like so many others, my grandfather supplemented his winter fishing with summer farming. He owned a little livestock, while potatoes, carrots, fish and doses of cod liver oil constituted the staples of our diet. Although these basics kept body and soul together, I developed digestive problems with the accompanying bloated stomach, plus anemia. These symptoms went mostly untreated during the war as doctors' appointments were scarcer than hens' teeth to come by—especially in a rural setting. What little flour we had was combined with mysterious ingredients such as tree bark. Watching "baked" bread emerge from the oven was an engrossing spectacle. With the absolute minimum amount of flour, only a little crust had formed, and the insides of the loaf just seeped out in an independent mass. It was only much later in the war, really towards the end, that children in Northern Norway received care packages: soup ingredients from Sweden and *spekepølse,* a salty lunchmeat, from Denmark, the latter a new and sensational treat!

Bodø was bombed heavily by the Luftwaffe on 27 May 1940, the date of our initial evacuation. The town was reduced to ruins. Only skeletal structures remained of places we had been familiar with before. During the devastation, we heard the bombing, and the clear night sky was illuminated by the flaming buildings. In addition, our area teemed with German soldiers. Everywhere we turned, there they were: marching along, helmeted, bayonets affixed to their rifles. I surely was not alone in feeling intimidated by these invaders. Should we encounter them on the road as they marched by, they expected even the children to raise their right arm in salute and proclaim: "Heil Hitler"! Having to yield to them on the road as well as salute was enough to make anyone shake in their boots!

The Germans had established a base near our house, partly built into the hillside. I had to pass by this on my way to school, until they took over even our modest two-room schoolhouse later on. Education continued after a fashion. Classes were held in private homes. We had the same two teachers year after year, and these were excellent.

Not only did they impart whatever academic knowledge they could under very trying circumstances, but they did their best to prepare us to enter the work force, which was expected of us. For me as for countless others, continuing education was postponed, but I did make up for it later.

The Germans had taken many prisoners of war and some of these fashioned wooden figurines of chickens and roosters for us children, hoping for a little food in return. One Polish prisoner in particular, from Warsaw, had learned a little Norwegian. He was a kind man and told me I reminded him of his daughter. Once as part of a transport convoy, he threw a loaf of bread my way—real bread! Another time he gave me a little candy. When he was shipped out near the end of the war, I felt very sad when I heard that the ship he was on had been sunk.

Although life went on as best it could in Northern Norway, our communication with the outside world was virtually nil. We didn't learn of the intense naval battles in Narvik during the first two months of the war until months later. Likewise we were kept in the dark about events on the global scale. We might as well have existed in a vacuum! All over Norway, radios were confiscated and our area was no exception. Our only and limited access to news was at the home of my grandmother's cousin, a gardener by trade for the city of Bodø. His radio had remained intact, concealed under a black fabric covering. What we didn't suspect, was that this family member actually had become a spy on behalf of the Norwegian Underground, reporting on

German activities. Outwardly, however, he appeared to collaborate with the Germans, thereby becoming despised and hated by his own kind. Meanwhile his daughters added insult to injury by flirting with the German soldiers. We could only conclude that it was his outward relations with the Germans that kept them from looking more closely under his radio's black shroud. After the war, this relative's name was cleared and he was awarded several medals for his courage.

The Germans began retreating from Finnmark in Northern Norway as of the winter of 1944 and by the spring of 1945, their trucks and tanks were rolling into Bodø. At one point they parked vehicles in front of our home and demanded to stay with us, which four of them did for several days. One of the men was a high-ranking officer with a nasty disposition along with an icy stare. I stared right back. Even though by now it was clear to all that Germany had lost the war, their arrogance, as personified by this officer, was just as entrenched as ever. I could only feel hatred for the whole lot of them.

What a contrast it was instead, when Allied soldiers began arriving! British and Norwegian forces, handed out canned meat—nothing fancier than Spam, but we thought it was wonderful. In addition we had our first encounter with the exotic banana fruit! By 8 May, 1945, the church bells began to peal, and everyone spontaneously streamed towards the church, as did my grandparents and my fifteen-year-old self. Old and young alike commuted on foot as there were no private vehicles or public transportation of any kind. This impediment was overlooked as we were a jubilant crowd. Finally we were free again! We had all taken out our Norwegian flags from their hiding places. We even began to hope for the return of our father, who did in fact come back to us by the summer of 1945.

NORTHERN NORWAY:
1940—At the Center of the World

Exhibit, Norway's Resistance Museum at Akershus, Oslo;
submitted by Ron Petersen

German boots trample throughout Europe
The war people fly towards the North
Towards the Borderland
German bombs fall on Kirkenes
May 4th and June 2nd, 1940

The Reich Commissioner Terboven
hoists the German flag in Kirkenes June 17th
A warning for the East

The occupation troops march
During the autumn of 1940 and winter of 1941
masses of soldiers head toward the border
Finnmark is filled with warriors

In Finland a wall of men stand
from the Finnish Bay to the Varanger Fjord
475 000 Finns—200 000 Germans
Brothers in arms

The World War has arrived in the Borderland

NORTHERN NORWAY: HAMMERFEST

by Randi Brox and Astri Grieg Fry

I was born Randi Ingebrigtsen in Tromsø in 1935, but grew up in Hammerfest, Finnmark. My father worked for the Finnmarks Fylkesrederi og Ruteselskap (FFR), a ferry and bus service in those parts still in operation today. We lived a very simple life in Hammerfest. The town's distinguishing features are its port and deep harbor. Hence shipping is the lifeline connecting the mainland to the islands dotting the coastline. Then, due to the Gulf Stream, the area is ice-free most of the time, despite its location extremely far north of the Arctic Circle. These assets, however, became liabilities for us in 1940 when the Germans suddenly invaded Norway. The ice-free, deep fjords were ideal places for the concealment of large warships and submarines. From these positions, the Nazis intended to dominate the northern seas.

At the onset of the war I was five, and we lived in a ground floor apartment between some German barracks on one side and the church's cemetery on the other. In addition to erecting barracks for the thousands of German troops pouring into Norway, the Germans confiscated buildings such as schools and whatever else they decided they needed. Food was rationed, but we did have access to fish and could subsist on that. One uncle had a farm in the Tromsø area, and he supplemented our diet with sacks of potatoes, and possibly carrots and turnips. New clothing during the war was a rare event. When that did occur, a seamstress came to people's homes, bringing her sewing machine and performing her work onsite. As to footwear, fortunate indeed were those who owned *komager* or *skaller*, those expensive but wonderful Lapp shoes or boots made of reindeer skin or fur, respectively. We kids loved wearing them. They were colorful, lightweight and, lined with dried grass for extra insulation, perfect for keeping the wearer's feet toasty warm when walking on the subzero, powdery snow.

Still as a small child, out on my own one day, I saw a German ship enter our harbor. It had been torpedoed, and it sank. Next there were soldiers flailing about in the seawater. Later a number of their bodies were carried up to the churchyard. Of the buildings there at that time, only the churchyard chapel remained untouched and to this day still stands. However, this is where any number of German soldiers found their final resting place, their graves unmarked.

The Allies torpedoed both German ships and Norwegian vessels so the latter wouldn't be appropriated by the Nazis. Many of these, however, actually belonged to the Norwegian merchant fleet, vital to the transport of food, mail and cargo in general, along the coastal towns and the remoter island communities. My father as a ship captain would determine whether or not to set out to provide this essential service, braving stormy weather conditions in a relatively small ship. Many years later, I was in Stavanger visiting a friend. Purely by chance in a small tobacco store, when the tobacconist heard my Northern Norwegian dialect, he asked in like speech: "Did I know Captain

Ingebrigtsen?" "He was my father," I replied. "He was my hero!" exclaimed my new-found friend, "for the way he delivered vital supplies in those parts, while braving stormy seas, not to mention the warring Germans and Allies!"

And brave my father was, attacked four times while at sea. Torpedoes sank his vessel out from under him and his crew, and he was a seaman who couldn't swim. It seemed as if the ships and vessels under fire shrank in size in the wake of those early naval battles—evidently the larger and more important were the first to be targeted. Besides torpedoing at sea, there was bombing inland. Sirens went off at any time of day or night in Hammerfest, which occasionally was bombed by the Allies. We had to be prepared to run for shelter. However, most of the bombing was to the east of us. Kirkenes close to the Russian border was heavily bombed. The Kirkenes inhabitants hid in actual bomb shelters. In our area we took refuge in basements.

During the war, there were very few radios left in Hammerfest. My family had no radio and anyway the Germans banned our use of them. However, my father had access to a concealed radio and knew about important events like the Normandy invasion later on in the war. Adults had to watch what was said at home as children might repeat their parents' objections to this new regime within earshot of the Germans.

Many of the Germans soldiers were friendly towards us Norwegian civilians, which we thought was surprising. Many were quite young and still in their late teens. My mother, normally a friendly soul, gave them short shrift, however. For example, some offered greetings from her sister's son. She didn't fall for it, as he had been a radio operator and was imprisoned for his anti-Nazi activities. Some of the soldiers renewed their supplies of fresh water at our house, and when they came knocking, she insisted they check their weapons at the door. They did. They also knew they were headed for the Russian Front, and my mother maintained they would be unlikely to return. They, on the other hand, were proud to be going there and confident of victory. Nevertheless, once they were deployed eastward, we never saw them again.

Other friendly German overtures had disastrous effects. We personally knew of one young girl who married a German soldier who later was killed during the war. She took their baby and went to live in Germany. She knew that she and her offspring would be ostracized in post-war Norway for her relations with the enemy.

The Germans took many Russians prisoners and in our area established a fairly small prison camp where I saw them when they were outdoors. Being so relatively close to the border, we had mixed feelings about the Russians. If they came into Norway to liberate us from the German occupation, would they stay and take over? We felt caught between these two major forces. It would be accurate to say there actually were three major forces to contend with in Northern Norway. The long, dark and bitterly cold winter made up the third element.

Being caught between these three forces came to a head during the final winter of the war: 1944-45. As stated

217

before, the Germans had invaded Norway suddenly and now in identical abrupt manner, they posted notices on telephone poles, ordering mandatory evacuation for all, and that the burning of buildings would commence effective immediately. This was no empty threat. The Germans burned designated sectors one at a time. However, before we left, taking only what we could carry, my shutterbug of a cousin was able to capture many spectacular photographs of this conflagration.

To speed up the evacuation, it was possible to sail southward as passengers on a ship under German control. My father refused this offer. We evacuated on a *skøyte*, a small fishing vessel, but adequate for our three-generational family. Onboard this vessel, we actually could have steered for England, where we had some relatives, but it was too dangerous to attempt this. My father set course for Mosjøen instead and from there we went by train to Trøndelag. Our trip aboard this boat lasted for several days. At first I sought refuge in the boat's hull, but quickly discovered that it felt even more unstable down there than up on deck. Once in Trøndelag we stayed with friends. This evacuation actually proved fortunate for us. Now our new home was on a farm, with dairy products added to our formerly sparse diet. I also began my education at this time, entering the half-day school system at the third grade level.

Of other people residing in Northern Norway, the indigenous Laplanders would have had few contacts south of the Arctic Circle. Therefore it was simpler for them to remain in the Arctic wilderness along with their tents and

218

their reindeer herds. There were likewise thousands of Norwegians who refused to leave, many of whom took shelter in caves during that ghastly winter.

Having forced the residents from their homes, the Germans followed through with their "scorched earth policy" to deter the advance of the Russian forces. Every town in Finnmark was burned systematically. They made a wasteland out of Northern Norway, and burned Kirkenes completely to the ground. This devastating finale of the German retreat in Norway was unique to its northern region.

Immediately after the war, the men returned first in order to begin the reconstruction of homes and towns. Oddly enough, former homeowners were compensated for the loss of their burned homes by post-war Germany—at least to some extent. However, my family did not qualify for this. Meanwhile, everyone returning lived in barracks as first and it was several years more before we were able to move into our very own future home.

THE SALT OF THE EARTH
by Rolf Mørch and Astri Grieg Fry

Ivar Dervo grew up as the oldest of three brothers and a sister on a tiny farm east of the Tana River in Northern Norway's Finnmark area. There they had a horse and only one cow during the winter half of the year, not being able to store more winter fodder for any additional livestock. At one point, the horse died, and Ivar's father went to Karasjok to buy a new one, returning after a nine days' absence. These were great distances to overcome, in other words.

In November of 1944, the Red Army crossed the border into Norway supported by its own Air Force. In addition, armament assistance from the US was transported by convoy over the North Atlantic to Murmansk. Residents in eastern Finnmark were ordered by the Germans to evacuate westward along with the Wehrmacht, on threat of death if this order was not followed.

However, because distances in Finnmark are vast and the German troops' attention was concentrated on their retreat, Ivar's parents decided that the whole family would seek safety in the hillside area approximately 1 km. from their home. They took along a tent. Since other families without any tent appeared, however, all the children stayed in the tent, whereas the adults had to manage as best they could out of doors that first night. The following day they all moved a little farther upstream where they constructed some shelter against the elements. Since the ground was frozen, it was impossible to seal the cracks and sides of their lean-tos. All the same, after a while they did risk starting a fire to heat their food, not to mention to warm themselves!

While they were at this hideout, they could observe a German patrol boat on the Tana River with crews going ashore on both sides of the river setting fire to all buildings and docks. Since it is quite dark even during the day in November this far north, they could see quite well how everything burned on the opposite side of the river, although it was more difficult to see what was happening on the eastern side where their own farm lay.

Meanwhile, the patrol boat turned around about level with their hiding place and then disappeared. (It turned out later that the boat crew had been ordered to scorch everything up to a certain map perimeter as the Wehrmacht had time for no more destruction.) While the families were in hiding, they could hear several deafening explosions. They realized that the Germans were blowing up the bridges in order to impede the advance of the Red Army as effectively as possible. At the same time, they concluded after barely a week that all German troops now probably were located well to the west of the Tana River. Now they could leave their hiding place and learn the fate of their own little farm. It too was completely burned, while the nearest farm a little farther upriver had been spared as it was outside the boundary according to the German order. Nevertheless they found something of value—most unexpectedly. In the ground, where the house had stood, there still remained their supply of salt used for food preservation. The salt had not burned!

Ivar and Paula are our friends and neighbors and when we visited them at their cabin located on one part of the original property in the summer of 2013, we had ample opportunity to survey the surroundings. We accompanied Ivar when he erected two wooden posts with the inscription "Camp, November '44," at the two locations where the families so long ago had gone into hiding. In that instance, we experienced peace and radiant midnight sun as opposed to continuous darkness and war.

As a result of Ivar's World War II experience, he was inspired to defend his country, and he did so by becoming a military career officer, ultimately rising to full colonel and then serving as the Norwegian military attache in Helsinki. Now he is a spry retiree, with whom most people would be hard pressed to keep up with on the cross country skiing trails. One of his brothers became a Home Guard captain in Finnmark.

A WORLD WAR II DIARY:
THE ROMANCE OF GUNNAR AND GERD STAVSETH
by Erik Stavseth and Astri Grieg Fry

My parents, Gunnar and Gerd Stavseth, high school sweethearts, may not have met at all had it not been for the German occupation of Norway in 1940. In fact, Gunnar had already graduated from Riis High School in the early '40s, but transferred to Gerd's school, Berg. Why? Well, so as to avoid being swept into the work force under Nazi control, allegedly under the alibi of "improving his *artium,*" his final high school diploma grades.

After the couple graduated in 1944, Gunnar subsequently left for Sweden to join the Norwegian police force there. In 1945 Gunnar's troop was ordered to ski through the Finland area to Kirkenes, thereby participating in the retaking of Finnmark in February of 1945. (This was in the wake of the German retreat, where they had burned Finnmark to the ground as a deterrent to the advancing Red Army.) One of Gerd's most cherished mementoes of this time was a diary that Gunnar kept while on this expedition, although this epoch was not without drama and danger. On 1 March, 1945, the entry reads: "Today offered a most welcome surprise: the arrival of your 17 January letter. (Needless to say, this was many years before the invention of the cell phone!) Now the moon shines pale and cold over the ruins and the stars, and the Northern lights almost compete in outshining each other. In the distance I hear the

223

Russians' monotonous campfire singing: now subdued, now louder. It is cold and the entire landscape appears as if bewitched. I wonder if I ever will come out of this alive. Tomorrow we will be heading west toward the Front. There are land mines everywhere and the probability for whichever man is leading the troop to be killed by a land mine is estimated at 90%."

Gunnar did not return from Northern Norway until July, 1945, and the couple were married in 1946. Gunnar continued in the military and eventually became an Air Force captain. In 1953 he was sent to the US for training in New Mexico. When he returned that same year, he became crippled by polio and died a short time later.

And so Gerd was widowed already in 1953, but Gunnar's diary provided her with much solace. She reread it often. Especially during her last years, it was constantly on her night stand.

I, Erik, Gunnar and Gerd's son, was born in 1950. Once Gerd began to work for Norske Shell, I was fortunate in that I lived with my maternal grandparents in Bergen until I was six. My grandfather, Einar Magnus was a Lt. Colonel in the Coast Guard Artillery. Gerd stayed with Norske Shell her entire working career, until she retired in 1988. She had many valued co-workers from this time, but many of them are now gone.

Chapter 5: Norway and Beyond

" LET THEM LOOK TO NORWAY"
—Public Papers of the Presidents of the United States

In 1942, a submarine chaser, re-christened the HNoMS King Haakon VII, was presented to the Norwegian Navy by President Roosevelt. It was at this presentation that the president gave his "Look to Norway" remarks, followed by remarks by the crown princess.

"If there is anyone who still wonders why this war is being fought, let him look to Norway," said President Roosevelt. "If there is anyone who has any delusions that this war could have been averted, let him look to Norway; and if there is anyone who doubts the democratic will to win, again I say, let him look to Norway."

Crown Princess Martha also had a few words to say: "The beautiful and generous words just expressed by you, Mr. President, will ultimately find their way to every Norwegian home. Yes, to everywhere on this globe where Norwegian men and women are praying and working and fighting to regard the free and happy Norway. All our deepest thanks."

A WARTIME SEPARATION
by Sidsel Tompkins

This story begins in 1933. Shortly after my parents' marriage, my father, Harald Hansen of Larvik, Norway, got a job on the ship *Kong Sigurd*, belonging to Det Sønnenfjeld's Norske Dampkipsselskap. The *Kong Sigurd* sailed between Kristiansand and Hamburg, Germany. Harald signed on as a sailor. The ship carried all sorts of different loads: automobiles from Germany, flour, sugar and coffee. These trips were short, and he was able to come home frequently. The Oslo-Bremen route brought him home every two weeks and he was able to spend a night or two at home before taking off again. These trips on *Kong Sigurd* continued until 1939.

On September 3, 1939 war was declared between England and Germany. The *Kong Sigurd* was in Kristiansand at the time and waited there a week, anticipating orders from headquarters. They were told to lay up in Oslo, as there was to be no trade with Germany. Harald went home for a few weeks and then got a job on the *California Express,* a fruit express line owned in Arendal, Norway. At that time, Harald thought he would be away for about 18 months. Actually, it turned out to be six years and three months before he returned.

The *California Express* was a banana boat. It went through Panama bringing supplies to the Canal Zone and from there to Seattle. The United States was not at that time in the war, not until December, 1941.

The effect of the Second World War on Norway was that, as an occupied country, Norway was not allowed contact with the Allied countries. It was against the law for Norwegians to leave Norway. Harald got off the *California Express* in Seattle and was essentially stranded there. He was unable to return to Norway. In 1941, he got a visa to emigrate in Seattle and became a Seattle resident.

Having left his wife, Esther, and six-year-old daughter, Inger Marie, in Larvik, Harald had no idea how long the war might separate his family. He investigated plans to get them out of Norway. There was a route used over Northern Russia, an area called Petsamo. The Crown Princess of Norway and family left Norway through that route and stayed in safety during the war years in the United States. But plans for using that route did not work out for Harald.

In Seattle, Harald was lucky to get a job with a local builder. One day when waiting for a bus in the Seattle rain, a car stopped and offered him a ride. The driver turned out to be a supervisor for the Port Ashton Packing Company. By the time the ride was over, Harald was persuaded to sign up for the Alaska fishing season with Port Ashton. This was the beginning of a new career for Harald, being a marine carpenter during the winter, and working as a cannery tender captain in Alaska during the spring and summer months.

It must have been very difficult to maintain a relationship with his family during such a separation. Regular mail between Seattle and Norway slowed to a trickle in 1940 and stopped entirely in 1941. The Red Cross helped families communicate after this time. A Red Cross Message took 6 months, and the reply written at the bottom of the message would take another 6 months to get back. The message could contain no more than 25 words and could say nothing about work or anything considered controversial.

With a spouse at sea off and on since the beginning of their marriage, my mother developed a high degree of self-reliance. But it had to be a lonely time for her and my sister, Inger Marie. They were lucky to have a strong, supportive extended family nearby in Larvik and Hedrum in Vestfold. Esther's family had a farm, and so they were regularly supplied with food. They lived in an upstairs apartment in a house next door to Nanset School. German forces took over the school, and they could look out their window and watch the soldiers marching in the school yard. Esther had hidden a radio in the attic and they would listen nightly to news of the outside world in secret, as radios were forbidden. After a while, the landlord got nervous and asked her to get rid of the radio.

Esther took in sewing to help make ends meet, as Harald was not permitted to send money to his family. Rationing was restrictive. Ordinary items like flour were extended with other grains so bread turned out heavy and unsavory. Mothers with small children were able to get some white flour on their rationing card. Children were given cod liver oil at school. Esther sent Inger Marie to school with the biggest spoon she could find for her daily ration. Sugar was highly prized and scarce. Esther remembered being unable to buy coffee, (a keenly felt deprivation for a Norwegian) and burning chicory or rye as a substitute. She also told of walking downtown and observing German soldiers spreading butter on chocolate bars and eating them to taunt hungry townspeople.

Many townspeople were secretly involved in the Resistance Movement. Esther did not know that one of her brothers had been deeply into the Resistance until, after the war, he asked her to sew a special patch on his jacket.

May 8, 1945 was a day of elation and jubilation in Larvik. The Germans had surrendered and the town once again belonged to the Norwegians. Nine days later, May 17th, Constitution Day was celebrated in Larvik's renowned beech forest, Bøkeskogen, in a heady rush of patriotism and exhilaration. Many households framed a picture of German troops handing over Akershus Fortress in Oslo to Norwegian forces. This picture became symbolic of national pride and held a place of honor on many walls for years.

Although the war was over, Harald had a hard time connecting with Norway. Esther got a letter at the end of July. He got an answer in August. At the end of the Alaska fishing season, he traveled to the East Coast, where he got a job that paid one krone a month on the ship *Kronprinsen*. Essentially it meant free passage to Norway, available to him as a seaman on Norwegian ships.

Harald arrived in Oslo on October 25, 1945. The extended family was there to meet him. Inger Marie had been six years old when he left Norway and she was now twelve. She was thrilled to get to know this father of whom she had only dim memories. Although feelings were not often discussed openly by members of their generation, for my parents it had to be like getting to re-acquainted with a new partner and establishing a whole new relationship.

There was much to catch up on. The family loved to hear about Seattle and Alaska, places they had never dreamed to visit. A favorite story was how tall the blueberry bushes grew in Alaska. Harald produced a picture of himself on a ladder picking blueberries. For Norwegians used to scrambling on the ground to pick, it became a family saying for anything that seemed an exaggeration: "That must be like the blueberries in Alaska."

Harald and Esther's second daughter, Sidsel, was born in August, 1946. In 1950, the family moved to Seattle as economic opportunities were much better there than in recovering Norway. They connected with Norwegian immigrants and organizations while maintaining strong ties with relatives and friends in Norway. They spoke Norwegian at home and returned "home" frequently as their finances improved. Norway was always home to them.

A NEW DIRECTION
by Sidsel Tompkins

In April 1940 my aunt Aase Johansen Faret was in Oslo, working as a nanny and housemaid for a family that lived in the upscale Holmenkollen district. She lived in, and her duties were caring for two young boys, 4 and 5 years old. Their father was an attorney. In addition to caring for the boys she helped with housework. She did not have to do any cooking as the family employed a cook. Aase came from a farm on the outskirts of Larvik, about 130 km. to the southwest. She was 20 years old and was enjoying her first taste of city life.

On April 9 in the morning, alarms sounded as German planes flew over Oslo, and troops took over the city. Aase was on an errand in town and when she returned to the house on Holmenkollen, she found the house deserted. There was no note or letter explaining where the family had gone. Unsure of what to do, she stayed in the house awaiting some word from her employers. There was no panic, as the occupation occurred peacefully. There was no bombing in Oslo or the surrounding area. After a day or so, some relatives of the family came to the house and moved in upstairs. They explained that the family had been alarmed and fled northward to a town where they had connections. Aase figured that her employment must be ended and so she returned to her own family in Larvik.

As it happened, she soon got another position working in the house of the poet Herman Wildenvey. He and his wife and daughter lived in the small town of Stavern, along the coast south of Larvik. Aase's duties were primarily housework, but she often was asked to help in the kitchen. Gisken Wildenvey asked Aase if she knew how to make *wienerbrød*, a rich Danish pastry. Aase was too intimidated to say no, although she had never tried baking anything so complicated. The pastry turned out disastrous, but Mrs. Wildenvey was gracious and didn't remark on it, though she never asked Aase to bake again. The war did not have a memorable impact on Aase's life in the poet's household. Life at Hergisheim, the Wildenvey home, was rural and peaceful. She was busy learning new skills and was not privy to what must have been intense political conversations between the Wildenveys and their circle of friends.

Within a year or so, Aase got a new job helping in a general store in Larvik. As before, her duties included keeping house as well as waiting on customers when needed. In the store, everything was rationed, even milk and herring. Margarine had to be mixed with potatoes to stretch it out. Meat was very strictly rationed. Aase enjoyed her work at the store and she was provided with room and board. The lady in charge, Frøken Treveland, remarked on Aase's skill and speed with her duties. She said that they must have the cleanest house in Larvik. She also thought that Aase was capable of much more than being a store clerk and a housekeeper. She sponsored Aase and encouraged her to apply for nurse's training in Tønsberg.

With Frøken Treveland's recommendation, Aase

was accepted for nurse's training which lasted three years and three months during the war years. She was trained at Tønsberg Hospital and graduated as a Red Cross nurse in October, 1947.

After the war was over, several concentration camp survivors were sent to the hospital to recover. They were ill and badly emaciated. Some were Russians who stayed in the hospital for four to five weeks. Aase was shocked to see their condition and became friends with several of the patients.

Her training completed, she continued working at Tønsberg Hospital until her sister persuaded her to emigrate to America. She joined her sister in Seattle and was hired as an RN at Swedish Hospital. Her Norwegian training served her well.

A WARTIME CHILDHOOD IN MANCHESTER, ENGLAND

by Albert Crompton, George Spacey and Astri Grieg Fry

When World War II first broke out in England, I was only two and a half and hardly took up much space in my family's 400 square foot house. Conveniences were minimal. We had cold water running through lead pipes (banned in more modern times), no hot water, no electricity and the bathroom was a separate outside structure. We did, however, have gas lighting with upside-down mantles and a radio. Food during the war was plain; that is, if eating horse meat is anyone's idea of plain. Overall, food consumption was dictated by the rationing books. Chicken and dairy products were doled out in limited quantities, and dinner menus were stretched into mostly soup and stew offerings.

The war in England didn't really heat up until a few years later, about 1942 when the bombing started. I was five to six years old during the most intense bombing phase. We lived fifteen to twenty miles from industrial Manchester on the outskirts of the heaviest bombing concentrated there, but vulnerable to its peripheral effects. Locally there were two mainline railroad tracks one quarter of a mile apart, maintained by hundreds of Italian prisoners of war. We lived right in-between these tracks. There was also a gun cotton factory producing the material used in firing shells. Like the railroad lines, this factory was a natural key target. Inevitably, the Luftwaffe dropped bombs. Once, missing their intended local targets, they

234

instead demolished a row of houses, even though the second bomb dropped failed to detonate. Emerging from the shelter one morning, we saw that these houses had been reduced to nothing but rubble and dust from the bomb explosion. All the windows had been blown out of the buildings in the adjacent two streets.

Some of the railroad tracks spanned bridges, and another time we saw a train coach hanging down over the side of the bridge, derailed by bombing. Primarily, airfields were targets, but cities also were bombed for a demoralizing effect on military personnel and civilians alike. This, however, only served to make the British population more determined than ever to resist the German aggressors.

If you were out during the day, there was always the chance of being caught in the sights of a German plane returning from a raid. They had only to cross the English Channel's twenty-mile span and they would be "home again" in occupied France. Homeward bound, they regularly used up their remaining ammunition to lessen weight, strafing people as well as targets and flying so low that you even could see the pilot's face,.

For years then we spent countless nights seeking refuge from the unrelenting bombing. We youngsters were taught by adults to run alongside buildings as we dashed to the shelter. Although it was frightening, we didn't really question the situation, but accepted this as the status quo. The older generations shielded us from its grim reality, that above ground, cities might be ablaze from the effects of the raids. In the shelter, there were bunkbeds for the kids. Otherwise the women sat up all night, doing whatever they could to get through the terror—talking to each other, drinking tea, knitting—until sirens sounded the all clear and we all could emerge above ground once again.

During the war years, we were a society of children, women, grandparents and a few wardens, those men who had been turned down for active duty. We grew close to these mentors—our dads and all other able-bodied men being absent from our lives. Even though my first school was obliterated by bombs, I did begin attending school as scheduled and, like my classmates and teachers, daily carried my gas mask to and fro. The wardens and the teachers would tell us when it was necessary to don them during the air raids. This happened several times. Being children, we looked for opportunities to play and explore, despite living in a war zone. Once, as mentioned earlier, a 500 lb. bomb had been dropped, but not exploded. The wardens chased us away from the vicinity. Later it was defused and we could play on it. We would look for incendiary bombs being taught by the wardens which were safe to pick up. Once a pile of shells absorbed our attention so completely that we "missed" three days of school.

Everyone we knew lost family members during the war. One of my uncles was a prisoner of war on a Japanese ship which sank. The Japanese locked all their prisoners in the hold so that they could not possibly survive. My dad, however, was more fortunate. He had left in 1939, returning to us in 1945 at war's end. At no time during these years had we seen him, nor did we even know where he was. Later he could tell us he was stationed on the coast, as a gunner firing anti-aircraft shells from aircraft guns. I was nine when he returned, walking home with other soldiers. Even though I hadn't set eyes on him for over five years, I said to the others with me: "That's our dad!"

And it was.

KOMPANI LINGE
by Sidsel Sandvik and Astri Grieg Fry

Martin Linge, among the first to resist the German occupation of Norway, soon began recruiting men into the Norwegian Independent Company operating in England. After he was killed in action against the Germans in Norway in December 1941, the Company was renamed in his honor, becoming Kompani Linge.

In back on left, King Haakon VII and Prof. Leif Tronstad on right; in front on left, Capt. Harald Sandvik and Crown Prince Olav on right in 1944 at Glemore Lodge, Scotland, the Kompani Linge training facility. Source and photo: Norway's Resistance Museum, Akershus, Oslo.

After 1942 the Company was run on a joint Norwegian-British basis and from 1943-44, Harald Sandvik was its commander at the special training school

238

in Scotland, carrying on the training of radio operators, saboteurs, small arms instructors and the leaders of clandestine fighting groups. Nor was psychological warfare instruction overlooked.

Prior to taking over the Kompani Linge, Harald had traveled in the USA and Canada during 1942-1943 on behalf of the Ministry of Information, speaking to a Norwegian-American audience regarding the Resistance Movement in Norway.

Much later, Harald recorded his wartime experiences in two publications: Frigjøringen av Finnmark 1944–1945 (The Liberating of Finnmark) in 1975, and Krigsår: med Kompani Linge i trening og kamp (War Years: With the Linge Company in Training and Battle) in 1979.

The following documents cover Harald's "Agreement required by the Department of Defense" upon his arrival in England after fleeing Norway via Sweden in 1942, the "Report on the Fyresdal Meeting" and the "Report to the Foreign Office by Bonzo." These documents have been donated to Norway's Resistance Museum's Archives at Akershus, Oslo, by Harald's daughter, Sidsel Sandvik.

The Department of Defense.

TO NEW ARRIVALS FROM NORWAY

Messages from Norway constantly provide intelligence stating that at home our countrymen's lives are endangered through careless talk beyond the country's borders.

The Department of Defense finds it necessary to enforce the greatest security regarding references to conditions and of persons in Norway. It is especially emphasized that it is strictly forbidden to provide information as to where, aided by whom, and in which manner you have left Norway. This ban does not only include any publicizing through the press or radio broadcast, but also information which emerges in private conversations and in private letters,—in other words, all communication which can provide any outsider with knowledge of your flight or experiences in that connection.

Any violation of this ban may entail serious punishment.

<u>VIOLATION OF THIS BAN MAY EXPOSE YOU FAMILY AND FRIENDS TO TORTURE AND SUFFERING.</u>

===

I have received a copy of this document and confirm that I have familiarized myself with the ban regarding careless conversation, etc. regarding conditions and persons in Norway.

London,   21st November, 1942

....

Sandvik, Harald   [signed]

....

Full name, in printed letters   Signature

Translated from Norwegian by Astri Grieg Fry

240

REPORT ON THE FYRESDAL MEETING

At FO's request a meeting was arranged between JOHN OPSAHL and a representative from SL. According to the plan, JACOB, John's man in AUST-AGDER, should also have been present, but did not appear. It is not known why he failed to turn up. From SL ARILD attended the meeting, which was fixed for February 15 [1945] in FYRESDAL. ARILD came there at the time appointed, and was met by a courier from VARG, who took him to HANS, VARG's second in command. HARALD, the leader of VARG, was away and did not return before ARILD went back. Owing to a misunderstanding JOHN did not arrive at the meeting place until Saturday, February 17. He had been waiting at another place since the Tuesday evening. With him came NILS, his second in command in VEST-AGDER.

JOHN explained the situation in D.18 and his report is enclosed. A report on the series of arrests which took place at the beginning of November 1944 is also enclosed. As JOHN's report shows, he has now about 50 men on the moors in VEST-AGDER. He has not been able to form these men into cells, on account of the difficulties as regards supplies in the district, but has them in ones or twos round about in huts. A few have been placed at farms. In JOHN's opinion he has to act on the principle of making himself as independent as possible of the people in the neighborhood of the garrisons which have been planned, as it has proved to be difficult to prevent the Nazis in the district from learning about the food supplies, if these are to be arranged through the people in the district. An essential

241

condition for being able to collect the men in large garrisons is that some of the supplies should be obtained direct from UK and from SL's supply organization. This is arranged by forwarding goods to business addresses in VEST-AGDER, and the first consignment will leave in the course of a few days. JOHN also expected that the supplies from UK would arrive at the first opportunity.

It is the intention to form the men into cells, each of five or six men, as soon as the supplies have been arranged. The Quarters available are mostly small primitive *seter* buildings, mountain dairies, as he is dependent on the supply of wood, etc. to the huts. As soon as the cells have been formed, he will begin to give instructions in the use of arms and in demolition tactics, in addition to training these men as troop leaders and section leaders, with a view to using the personnel of these cells to form the core of the build-up of the district. JOHN was very satisfied with the men he had got. They were all very strong, well trained men, very suitable for cell work. The district which has been allotted to him is extensive, with few roads, and therefore all transports will be long and laborious. He considers it necessary, therefore, to only use men he knows, who can stand hard work. JOHN had not yet seen the main directive from SL to DS and he was therefore given a copy of it, with a list of the targets in D.18. In proportion to the number of targets, the forces in AUST- and VEST-AGDER are too small to enable an effective defense of the targets to be undertaken. It was therefore decided that, as soon as the cells had been formed and the instruction work commenced, JOHN should establish a cautious connection with the sections in the district which were still intact. He estimated that there was a total of about 500 men in AUST- and VEST-AGDER, to which the forces in NISSEDAL and FYRESDAL could be added. VARG had, by arrangement, taken over the organizing and instructional work in NISSEDAL and FYRESDAL. It is not known exactly how many men were available there, but it was thought about 170. These men can be employed for the defense of HØGEFOSS power station. In addition to the arms at the disposal of VARG, JOHN estimates that he has arms for 250 men in AUST- and VEST-AGDER.

As JACOB did not attend the meeting, ARILD received information from JOHN about what he knew about the conditions in AUST-AGDER. JACOB's cell, consisting of 6-8 men, is engaged on the reception of drops from aircraft, and the provision of quarters in connection with the further work in the district when the conditions permit of a development. See also JOHN's report. JOHN was very interested in getting home capable and powerful men belonging to the district, who are now living in Sweden or the UK, but he laid great stress on the point that it was necessary that only men should be considered who were fitted for a laborious life in the field. Among the people whom he would particularly like to see return were JOHAN BARTH, LEIF DAHLEN, Inspector SAAGHUS, Sergeant KONRAD EVENSEN, OLA LØLAND and LACKEN AANENSEN.

JOHN appeared to be rather depressed over the unfortunate "roll-up" in D.18, but on the other hand he was very keen on starting the cell work, if only the supplies could be satisfactorily arranged. We agreed to establish a monthly courier service from SL to D.18, and the first courier will leave about March 15. ARILD tried to get HANS in VARG to make a report about his work, but he held the view that he could not do so without HARALD's permission. It was therefore decided to ask FO if a report should be made, and a reply in the affirmative was received. The same day, however, there came a warning about German forces being on their way up into the mountains, and HANS thought that his duties would not permit him to devote any time to making reports. He said he would have to go round at once to give warnings, and also to keep his man intact. After a wait of 1 1/2 hours there came a message to say that HANS would be away for an indefinite time. ARILD then considered that he could not postpone his journey home any longer, and left without obtaining any further knowledge of VARG's work.

PS: About a fortnight after the FYRESDAL meeting it was decided, at a meeting with BIRGER in SUNSHINE, that JOHN could send about 20 of his men to BONZO, to take a course of some duration, with special reference to the training of troop leaders and section leaders. A message about this will be sent to JOHN by courier. We are requesting JOHN to arrange with FL the technical details about making contact.

244

REPORT TO F.O. FROM BONZO
dated March 10, 1945

The military organization work has entered on a new and more active phase. I will make a short report, with special reference to the training which has been started.

Late last autumn the section leaders were given instructions by Tor Halvorsen in the use of weapons. They were also given arms for their personal protection. An extended training for all members of the sections was commenced at the beginning of February this year. Until this the members had only known the organization as a remote conception. The training has been carried out by sections, in accordance with a written programme. All the men have been instructed in the use of every weapon, and exercises in military tasks have been included.

The training conditions in the district are very good, and we have been able to test all the arms for the sections by actual firing practice. There are large uninhabited areas here, and the firing has not been heard by outsiders.

The weapons of the sections have been stored in the section depots, which only the section leader knows of, but now I am going to let each man have his own weapon and conceal it himself.

The experiences obtained from the training were very good. The men have become more steady. There have been no cases of careless talk on the part of the members of the organization. The training has been followed with great

245

keenness, and the men have displayed a good military bearing. Rigorous security regulations have been drawn up; they were read aloud by the section leaders during the training, and the men have obeyed them strictly.

The first phase of the training has now been concluded. The section leaders are not able to teach the men anything more.

In order to increase the fighting efficient of the detachment, I have now taken about 15 section leaders into the mountains, to give them a three weeks' course in section-leading and instructional work. They left their homes for this period under various excuses. The training could not be carried out while they were living at home, as it would in that case have been noticed. This training should increase the detachment's efficiency considerably, and remedy our greatest weakness, which was the boys' lack of training. I enclose the programme for the course. The plan is certainly an ambitious one for three weeks, but I hope to be able to get through it by the appointed time, with the capable instructors I have. A fixed order of the day has been drawn up, and great emphasis will be placed on discipline and a soldierly bearing.

The field equipment of the sections has been noted down on paper, and it is also a great boon to get an opportunity of giving it a practical test (see enclosure).

At the termination of the course I will prepare a further plan for the training of larger forces in BA 2, on the basis of the experience gained.

The security conditions are good, although I have had to depart from some regulations, in order to be able to complete the training. The troop and the sections have so far been closed cells, so I have not been able to prevent the section leaders from getting to know one another. I think that it is justifiable, however, at this period of time, to cancel some security regulations, for the benefit of the training. I have taken the natural consequences of this, and have given the troop leaders orders that they may use their weapons to prevent the arrest of any of our men, if such an action should be necessary. As the work has now acquired a more solid framework, I have changed from verbal to written instructions. If I can avoid coming into contact with other military groups, there is every reason to believe that the work will proceed without any interference from the enemy. Even the slender contact which I have with Sunshine is a weakness. Julius has been informed, via Einar, of some of my internal conditions. If anything goes wrong in Sunshine's neighboring area, I believe that I could manage to isolate it from here, though I am not sure. People have been posted in the villages to listen to gossip and to make up counter-rumors, but I have only been obliged to frighten people who have been talkative on three solitary occasions in two year. This has always proved effective.

The large number of drops that have taken place have gone well.

The warning system works well. It will not be extended to make it effective at night, when the exchanges are closed.

Generally speaking the rather slack inner security has been replaced by a more strict outer security, by removing as many contacts as possible to the outside.

The staff work is working well, and has now been solidly built up. I have been very fortunate with the officers and NCOs who have joined me. They are now very competent instructors. They will all form a very welcome addition to the officers and NCOs during the fighting, and it is my intention to use them as troop leaders, if they are not entrusted with more important tasks.

I will give a brief resume of the troops, which I have already telegraphed.

The smallest operative unit is the troop. Each troop has four to five sections of ten men. One of them is a pioneer section. All are ski formations. We are now working on the formation of a ski-toboggan supply service for each group. A company consists of three troops. Only one company is being made ready for action at present. I enclose a plan for the formation and armament of the section. All infantry sections are JG sections. The weight of the weapons and equipment for the section has been reduced to the minimum permissible.

The mobilization stations are in the areas at ARNE, THORE AND TROND. Superfluous material is now being driven down near to the road, over the snow.

The written mobilization orders and orders and situation orders have been worked out with every troop leader doing duty.

In accordance with the wish expressed by London by telegram, I will now, when we are approaching the time when the snows will have disappeared, prepare a suggestion for the capture of the fortresses in the area, by surprise. If a German occupation of the fortresses actually takes place, I shall, however, have to concentrate our strength at one place, with the limited forces available. An occupation of the fortresses by the enemy will not be possible, however, until the end of May. There is little snow this year on the west side, and many indications of an early spring, but the end of May is the very earliest at which the Germans will be able to open up the most low-lying roads, which are now covered with snow.

As regards BA, see the previous very detained telegram. Nothing has been changed in the principles which I then emphasized, but the hardest part of the winter has now gone by, and so the work will be less onerous. I will repeat one point in the telegram which I consider to be of very great importance. It is extremely dangerous to have two leaders in one area. They will constitute a breach of security for one another. The BA leader and the Milorg leader should be the same everywhere, not only with me. The conditions are so transparent that there has to be a natural explanation for every stranger who appears in the villages. Even a badly made ski track will lead to talk.

The food supplies are working well. I have enough flour for 100 men for two months, and an unlimited opportunity of procuring meat. Potatoes are the worst difficulty.

I am still living in BA.2 West, where the conditions are good, although there is only accommodation for about 20 men. If more BA.2 men arrive I shall have to move to BA.2 North, but shall not be able to live there without the villagers noticing it. I should have to use the farmers' *seters*, summertime dairies, and there would be talk. I believe that I should be able to prevent the talk spreading, however, I have men in the village who are very clever at preventing talk, and I think it would take a long time for the report to get further than the villages, but it would not succeed in the long run, of course. I should have to prepare to defend myself, if necessary, and experiences from outside indicate that the Germans hesitate to attack a well-armed position as long as possible.

I shall be able to procure food in addition to what is dropped by plane, even for forces of a considerable size, but more clothing and foot gear must be sent.

I wish to request that the order list should be strictly adhered to, if possible. I wish to thank for the good material I have received, but the lack of a small thing can lead to considerable inconvenience. For instance, we did not receive the lubricating oil ordered, and so damaged our motor generator. We only have one serviceable transmitter set, and would be helpless if that breaks down.

Einar has just asked me to take over about fifteen men from the neighboring district in the Sunshine area, and to intern them and train them in BA.2. I have agreed to do this. The security conditions for this district have been difficult for a considerable time and he hopes, by removing these men in good time, to be able to isolate those who remain.

I should like to write more, but I am afraid of giving information in this letter which might show where it comes from.

(Sgd) BONZO

IVAN, NATALIA AND MARIA
by *Maria Dmitrieva, Kristina Formuzal*
and Astri Grieg Fry

Before the onset of World War II in the Soviet Union, Stalin believed that his secret pact with Hitler would serve to protect his country. Therefore it was a universal shock to the Russians when, after invading Czechoslovakia and Poland, German troops crossed the Belarus border on June 22, 1941. Operation Barbarossa (the code name for Nazi Germany's planned invasion of the Soviet Union) had been put into effect. Having learned from the bitter defeat suffered by Napoleon, Hitler knew better than to launch an invasion during the Russian winter. Barbarossa was designed to conquer all of Russia brutally, swiftly and decisively within a five-month period, concluding by December 1941. Now the utmost priority of the German offensive was to paralyze the Soviet railway system. This was not only because the rail dimensions were wider than in Europe as one method of deterring European trains from entering Russian territory, but also because the railway system was the main means of military transportation, since the roads were suboptimal.

Hitler and Stalin had locked horns, triggering titanic events that affected millions of lives. The following story relates how the ensuing conflict shaped the destiny of the Iluhin family: Ivan Gerasimovich, born in 1914; his wife, Natalia; and their daughter, Maria, born in 1933 (who related the family's World War II experience to her granddaughter Kristina many decades later).

When World War II broke out, my grandmother, Maria, lived in Latvia with her parents, Ivan and Natalia. The first bombings happened during the night of June 21-22, 1941. Immediately, all men of military age were mobilized. Because of Latvia's proximity to the new front in eastern Europe, within hours a mandatory evacuation of civilians began. Natalia and Maria boarded a bus and were taken to the train station. They were not given time to pack or even say goodbye to Ivan. It was a matter of: "Take what you are wearing and go!" That night they were on a freight train (utilized to transport the maximum number of passengers), heading toward a Baltic seaport. However, in less than 24 hours German planes began bombing their train. Soviet aircraft were escorting the train, but were unable to provide adequate protection. All but the two first carriages were destroyed and caught fire. People were jumping out of them, hoping for the best, and there was no way of knowing what happened to them. Luckily, Natalia and Maria were in one of the intact carriages and made it to the Baltic Sea. From there they caught a ferry to Russia, then by land transport traveled into regions considered remote enough to ensure civilians' safety. Finally Natalia and Maria went on to Mihailovka, a small village near Orenburg, where Natalia's mother and brothers lived, remaining there throughout the duration of the war. The Germans never made it that far inland.

Ivan was mobilized on the same day his wife and daughter evacuated, but they did not know where he had been posted. During those five years of war there was no news from him.

The family reconnected in 1946. After Ivan was demobilized he went looking for them in Mihailovka. This was his best guess of where they could be if they had survived. His own family lived not too far away, in the same area, and where he and Natalia had met initially. He came and saw his brothers first, telling them about his life over the past six years. His division had been cut off by the Germans pretty quickly and they spent all five years of the war in the forests of occupied Belarus, practicing guerrilla warfare and surviving almost independently away from the main army, although aided by the local residents. However, he remained unable to get in touch with his family. After this family reunion of the brothers, he went to Mihailovka to find Natalia. When they met again, he asked Natalia and Maria to come and live with him in Brest, a city in Belarus, where he now had an apartment given by the government in recognition of his service. There the three of them could start a comfortable life anew.

Natalia said, "Nyet!"

It turned out that when Ivan shared his story with his brothers, one of them thought it was necessary to share a particular part of it with Natalia. He beat Ivan to Mihailovka and told Natalia that Ivan had had a romantic relationship with a Belarus woman, a nurse who saved him several times during the war. One may speculate as to what motivated this action, and also wonder what the future might have held for this family if this brother hadn't intervened?!

So Natalia chose to stay in Mihailovka. When it was clear that the marriage was over, Ivan asked if he could take Maria with him. He wanted to give her a chance to live in the city and go to a better school, so she could have a brighter future than the one she was likely to have in that tiny village. Natalia answered no again. Maria was her only daughter.

A few years later, however, Maria did make it to Brest. Once everyone was reassured that the war was well and truly over, Natalia's brothers convinced her that Maria would indeed be better off in the city.

Ivan remarried a woman named Vera, that very nurse with whom he survived the war. They had two daughters, the oldest of which survived infancy and became a good friend of Maria. They are close to this day.

A few years later, Natalia remarried too. She met a soldier who also fought in the war, and was still serving in the military. Together, they relocated to Bukhara in Uzbekistan. Now that Natalia also was living a comfortable life in the city, she wanted to get Maria back. Ivan, of course, objected, Bukhara being 4200 km away from Brest, but gave Maria the choice. She decided to go back to her mother, even though her father's family treated her very well. By then she was 16 years old.

Maria and her father remained close until he died, visiting each other whenever possible. Natalia and Ivan maintained an amicable relationship.

Ivan died in 1994 at the age of 80 from a heart attack. His wife Vera suffered a stroke shortly after, remained paralyzed and had a slow and painful demise.

Natalia's husband did not cope well with life after war. He was shell-shocked in one of the battles, and suffered from a severe post-traumatic stress disorder, which only manifested itself once he was back in a peaceful place. He was never violent, but suffered in silence and developed schizophrenia, from which he ultimately died. Natalia died in 1990 at the age of 76.

After my grandmother, Maria, had related this family story, I asked her if she blamed anyone for what happened to her family. She answered that, while she felt rather bitter and betrayed as a child, those feelings diminished as she grew older and understood the magnitude of what had happened. It was bigger than her mom and dad, and bigger than the breaking of marriage vows. It later had become clear that there were so many families in the same situation. Neither might have died during the war, but one (or both) partners started a new life just as a survival mechanism or because they had no idea if they would ever see their original spouse again. If they indeed were to meet after the war, often they did not know how to cope with these changed circumstances, which could feel more difficult and uncomfortable than if one of the partners had died.

Over time, Maria was able to visit her father every few years, and apparently she once took me along. It was in 1992, two years before Ivan died, and he even took us on a tour of the very forests where he once had fought the Germans, and told us war stories. Unfortunately, I could not take this in, as I was only five at the time. In contrast, I do remember clearly a beautiful porcelain ballerina figurine they had in their house.

ONE HUNDRED DAYS IN SAN VITTORE

by Walter Harold Schonbrun; introduction
by Nancy Schonbrun

How would a young man from Toledo, Ohio, who'd never traveled farther from home than Cleveland, adapt to life as a US Army radio operator on the Italian front in World War II? Among other ways, by learning to speak Italian from the residents of the town where he was stationed, by visiting some of the historical monuments like Pompeii he'd read about in his GI cultural guides, and by following his interest in classical music by attending opera performances as soon as theaters reopened. All of which meant that for my father, his tour of duty in Europe was more than the death and destruction he saw all around him, or the deprivation he sometimes personally experienced. It was also an introduction to a wider world that helped lead to a life of travel and a recognition that the world contained much more than he'd ever imagined as a young Jewish boy back in Ohio. As a continuation of his interest, he often recounted stories of his wartime experiences to my family at dinner. Because of that, places like small towns in Italy and the grand city of Paris seemed very real to me, even before I'd made my own way to Europe. Many years later, my father wrote the following story—perhaps because he'd lost most of his dinner audience by that time—about his stay in the small Italian town where he lived during the long siege of Monte Cassino.

258

After forty-three years one's memory tends to dim. Sometimes what really happened almost seems like a dream. At times, though, if something made a deep impression, recall is easy.

I remember quite well the one hundred—yes, it really was one hundred—days I lived in San Vittore Del Lazio, Italy. History tells us, and I will bear it out, that the Allied armies had a stalemate at Monte Cassino where the abbey was located.

While it is true that San Vittore was situated on a mountain, Monte Cassino was at a much higher level, and the Germans were looking down our throats. They had turned the abbey into a fortress.

The US Air Force came over in wave after wave to bomb the abbey. Every day, just like clockwork, the planes flew over the abbey, and the smoke rose.

I was attached to the 698th Field Artillery Battalion which had 255-mm. howitzers that were also employed in the attacks.

San Vittore was in many respects a typical small village built on the side of a mountain. The major difference between the prewar village and the time when I was there was that it was just populated with women, old men and children. The younger men, of course, were in the army or had fled. Many of the women and children had come down from Cassino and other places to be a bit farther from the front lines. I am not sure what the population was during the war. A 1980 census indicated a population of 2,142.

San Vittore had the usual fountain in a piazza where women and girls came each day for water. After filling up a jug or can, they hoisted it up onto a rag on the top of their heads. The fountain and the piazza were also used as a social meeting place.

Many of the houses in town had been bombed. It was a strange feeling when I went to church on a Sunday, as the church had no roof. The four walls were all that remained. If you looked up, all you saw was the sky. I wondered if, because of that, the people felt closer to God. At the very least, they must have felt that it was still Holy Ground. Was it their bombs or ours which had destroyed this church?

At times the villagers went to a makeshift church in a basement. Some of the religious artifacts had been salvaged from the original church. Lit candles at the altar were numerous. As a matter of fact, they supplied most of the light. Looking at the pained, worn faces of the women, one could readily see that they were praying for an end to the war, for food for their children and the safe return of their husbands.

As a radio operator in the army, once my stint on the radio was over, I had ample time to explore my surroundings. I explored the tiny town from one end to the other. I was constantly going up or down small streets. It was fun to discover a street that was a mere pathway where you could stretch your hands out and touch houses on both sides. As a result of my wandering I got to know practically all the townspeople. In the morning I received a *buongiorno* from everyone. It included a greeting from the ever-present old street sweeper with his broom made of twigs. The town was mostly rubble, but he kept sweeping.

The radio section lived on the second floor of a partially bombed out house. We pitched in a few liras apiece to pay a 12-year-old girl to sweep our room and straighten out our sleeping bags. It was a sort of luxury to have someone clean up for us.

One day while we were being shelled, Maria (every other girl in Italy seemed to be named Maria), I and other GIs ran into the basement of a house nearby. We found some civilians there who had sought shelter also. Maria started to cry and became hysterical. I slapped her face. Lo and behold, she stopped crying and calmed down. I think I had learned to do this from a movie I had seen.

In the public square one day I met Mario. He was ten years old and despite being a child of war, he was outwardly cheerful. Not only that, he was as smart as a whip, and stood out from the others. I attribute some of the Italian that I know to him. I'd ask Mario, "How do you say this in Italian?" and I'd point to an object. Then he would ask me, "How do you say it in English?" I could have adopted him on the spot.

In due time Mario took me home to meet his family. He was almost formal in presenting me to his mother, his 5-year-old brother Bruno, and the baby his mother was holding. Mario had given me the Italian name of Aldo, and I was know by everyone in town as Aldo.

I got to know that house as my home away from home. By American standards it was a hovel. It was one room of bare old bricks and crumbling cement. Despite its appearance, the place was alive and friendly, because a family lived there. Candlelight and flames from the small fireplace were the only illumination. The fireplace was also used for cooking.

On occasion I would bring the family some GI food, and their faces would light up. When Mario's mother offered me some of their food, I would just accept a small portion to be polite. It was very simple fare. I hated to take the food out of their mouths as food was so scarce. I just couldn't turn down the friendly offer to share their meal with me.

I spent a lot of time with Mario and his family . . . as a matter of fact, I became a part of the family. I think that I received more from them than I gave to them. With the war all around me, the family helped me maintain a semblance of sanity. After all, didn't I want to come home from the war, go back to my wife, have a home and children?

I've often wondered what happened to my "Italian family." If Mario survived the war, the hunger, etc, he would be twelve years older than my daughter Nancy.

One of the first things a GI outfit does when it moves into a new position is to dig a latrine. A hole is dug, a makeshift tarp put around it to give some semblance of privacy, and a wooden seat placed inside. At times it is a two-seater. Every once in a while, lime is thrown into the

262

pit. Orders are that you must use the "official latrine." It's more sanitary that way. You just can't go around doing it all over the place. Even though the war had messed up just about everything else, the regulations about the latrine were strict. Despite the official latrine, I found it more convenient to use the toilet I had found in an abandoned house. The toilet consisted of a niche in the wall about one foot deep by twenty inches wide. At the proper height was a marble slab, cold to the touch, with a hole. It worked by gravity. What a luxury! My own private toilet and no waiting in line. I even kept a few magazines there.

As a radio operator I had to take my turn as a forward observer. I had practically to crawl up a mountain with a portable radio, get a better sight on Monte Cassino, and relay fire orders back to the artillery units. I will never forget the stench of rotting human flesh on that mountainside. The vultures were numerous; it was not humanly possible to remove the bodies without being killed.

One day about five guys from the radio section were walking toward the chow truck for lunch, when the shells started to come in. We all ran toward a doorway to find shelter inside. Well, five people can't go through a doorway simultaneously. As a result we all hit our helmets together, and they went rolling down the street. After the shelling stopped, one fellow said, "Expletive—a guy could get killed around here!" With that remark we all stopped being shook up and started to laugh. The tension was gone.

Our objective had been to neutralize and capture Monto Cassino and the abbey which held up the advancing Allied forces. Ironically Monto Cassino never was taken. It had become a huge pile of rubble and was bypassed.

Some day I'd like to see San Vittore again. Hopefully it would not look the same. I doubt very much if I would know a single soul. You could be sure though, that if I walked down those streets, I'd see Mario in my mind's eye.

LETTER TO ELIZABETH HIRSCH SCHONBRUN
by Walter Harold Schonbrun; introduction
by Nancy Schonbrun

Another side of World War II I knew as a child, other than my father's excursions to opera and historical sites while he was on his European tour of duty, was more hidden because of its harrowing nature. Whenever I visited my grandparents in Toledo, Ohio, I would hear my grandparents, aunts, uncles, and parents whispering together in a mixture of Yiddish and English. The whispers were soft enough to conceal the details of what was being said, but that didn't hide the horrified emotions they produced. It was only as an adult that I learned from cousins who had fled their village in Slovakia to join the anti-Nazi partisans or to leave for more tolerant Bulgaria, before Nazis conquered their town in 1942, the fate of my relatives who weren't able to escape. Their mother, sisters, brothers, aunts, uncles, and cousins were sent, along with nearly all the Jews in Slovakia, to Auschwitz. Most were immediately killed. One cousin who survived, was so scarred by his brutal childhood that he committed suicide shortly after he reached America after the war. Another cousin who survived lived with such intense fear, sorrow, and survivor's guilt that his children, now with grandchildren of their own, still cry when the war is mentioned. My father, as the child of Jewish immigrants, was able to talk in Yiddish with Holocaust survivors he met in the wake of Germany's defeat. At that time the magnitude

265

of the horrors of the Nazi regime were just beginning to be known by outsiders, so much of what my father heard was entirely new to him. He wrote about his conversations to his young Norwegian-American wife back in Chicago in this letter.

Being the grandchild of Norwegian immigrants, my mother had lost touch with her family back in Norway, so she had no idea of how the war was affecting them. She was, however, dealing with the absence of her husband, whom she'd only married a year before he left for Europe, as well as her worries about her three brothers and two brothers-in-law who were all serving overseas. She spoke often to me of what it was like to live with worry and rationing during the war, but neither she nor my father ever spoke to me about this letter or the Holocaust in general. It was only after I'd lost them both that I found this letter in my parents' files and realized how much more they knew than they told me. Even without that, though, the war and the Holocaust had such a great indirect impact on me, despite having been born after it was over, that I will not watch movies or read books related to the war since its atrocities still feel very fresh in my mind.

Landsberg, Germany
10:30 p.m.
June 22, 1945
Dear Betty,
Believe it if you will. I believe it. Don't believe it because I am your husband and telling it to you. I know that you

266

won't think that my Jewish heredity has any reflection on my believing the following things.

I was in doubt at one time myself. I thought also, it was to a large degree just propaganda. I know how, and why, it was exploited. That doesn't mean that they are not facts. I have heard these things repeated over and over again. Sometimes from persons who had just heard about it. Sometimes from people who had actually experienced these things themselves.

I have heard of these things in Italy, in France, in Germany. Can everyone who told me these things be liars? A certain per cent of what I have heard, must be true. I have heard so *very* much, that much of these things, even if not all, must be true.

These things I can only put in cold type, and words. I can't tell you of the expressions or emotions of the people that have told me these things. You already must know what my reaction to these things would be. No, I don't think that I have much, if any, of an emotional reaction. Rather, I do believe that I understand just why these things happened, etc.

It was in a candle-lit room. The surroundings were rather crummy and the furniture was old and broken. The glass of beer that I was offered had a fly in it. My "hosts" were seven Jews whose ages ran from about seventeen to forty. These men (and I include the youngest when I say men, because they had really grown up mentally, if not physically, due to their experiences) came from about four different European countries. Many of the things that I am about to relate, will really sound incredible. In the words of one DP (displaced person): "Now that it is all over, we can hardly believe it ourselves. It all seems like a nightmare."

ARIYAH: Yes, there were times times when we were very hungry. At times, when we weren't fed anything at all by the Germans, we ate grass. And sometimes there just wasn't any grass.

SHMUEL: Once, a number of the people in the camp started to eat grass from the patch that was in one corner of the camp. The guard had a lot of sport out of shooting the people down, as they went toward the grass.

ARIYAH: And how many were the times that we were taken from our barracks (dingy and unheated as they were) and made to sleep in the snow? In the morning, I awoke to find others beside me, frozen to death.

ABRAHAM: This might sound so very unreal to you, but I have done this very thing myself. When there wasn't anything to eat because of the lack of water, we drank each others' urine. Please pardon me. That wasn't the half of it though. Once in a while, we were fed something very salty, and that made us very thirsty. *Then* they made sure not to give us any water!

SHMUEL: When the Germans first entered Poland, many men had to help burn their own families in a crematory!

HAROLD: I have heard that there were a few model camps in Germany that were shown to the Swiss delegates from the Red Cross. It that true?

SHMUEL: I was in one of the model camps for a short time. We were given good food, clean clothing, and the camp in general was cleaned up. After the delegates left, things went back to "normal" again. The food was taken away from us, and we suffered the same old things. Under the penalty of death, we had to go through this farce. The only Red Cross packages that we ever saw, were at these times.

ANOTHER MAN: See these marks on my body? They are from the lice. We were always covered with lice. When we were hungry enough—and when weren't we hungry?—we ate the lice.

ARIYAH: We often ate the meat from one of the persons that had died in the camp. Often as not, the person that had died, died from some disease. Can you believe that? We were like animals, I tell you. Like animals!

CHIAM: The fires in the crematory were always going. What an odor it spread throughout the camp! And to think, the SS troops held dances just a short distance away! Gasoline was used to keep the fires going. When they began to run out of gasoline, the fat from the cremated people was fed on the fire to keep it going.

It was us; us that had to feed the bodies to the fires in the crematory. Everything was done on a mass-production basis. Everything went like clockwork: bodies collected, fed in, fat and bones separated, etc.

Soap was made from the fat of those people that had gone to the crematory. Little cakes of soap! And the name of the soap was RIF. That stands for "Rhine Jewish Fat."

What sort of a mind could have thought to give us that soap to wash ourselves with? Being so very seldom clean, we used the soap. One just can't be sentimental. At least not when you have lice biting you all the time.

ARIYAH: Many were the times, when we wished that we could fall asleep, and just not wake up. For a very few, there was always just a spark of hope. Many of the people committed suicide. Every morning we were asked if we wanted to volunteer to go to the crematory. There were a lot of volunteers.

SHMUEL: I have seen with my own eyes, people that would just run up to the electrified barbed wire fence to die.

A RUSSIAN MAN: Remember (*speaking to the rest of his friends and myself*) the times that one of the guards would throw a piece of bread into a crowd and everyone would rush for it? People were killed in this manner also, as they killed each other in the attempt to get something to eat. It's hard to explain, but we were truly like animals.

HAROLD: Pardon me for writing down notes on what you are telling me, but there is so much, that I have to write it down in order to remember.

CHIAM: In that small notebook? You would need thousands of pieces of BIG paper to write everything down. And it would take many, many books to tell all about it. There are things that, now that it is all over, even we can hardly believe. That, despite the fact that we saw these things with our own eyes   Sometimes we didn't *want* to believe them.

ABRAHAM: We could tell you for days and days the things that happened to us, and the things we saw. I saw one guard take a baby out of its mother's arms and then pound the baby against a wall. They hung four or five people at a time, and let them hang there for days, so that we could see them. When people were first taken from their country, they were purposely separated to different camps. That wasn't enough for the Germans though, they told us that we would be able to see our relatives the next day just so that they could fool us, and tease us.

ANOTHER MAN: I was in a camp that sent work crews out every morning. The guards were *instructed* to come back with only a certain number. After work, men were picked out at random. You, you, you, you, etc, up against the wall over there! Then I saw 250 men shot down with machine guns. The remaining men had to wash the blood-splattered flesh off the wall. That's the way it was, day after day. No one knew just when he would be picked.

HAROLD: But why would they want to kill so many men when they could have been working for the Germans? There was a shortage of labor in Germany.

ANSWER: Men? Why, lives were very cheap. Thousands of new people were brought into the camp all the time. Besides, they were determined to exterminate us.

SHMUEL: Were it not for the Allied troops entering Germany, we all, in time, would have been exterminated. It was only that, that saved us. As the Americans approached the concentration camps, orders were given, to kill all of us just before the Germans withdrew. The Americans were too

271

quick for them, and the orders were not completely carried out.

In some cases, at certain camps, the Germans did start to kill off the people inside the camps. That is how many of us died at the very last minute.

ANOTHER POLE: Almost every morning, we woke up to find a few more dead people beside us. Sometimes I would shake someone next to me, to wake him up. After the first few shakes, I knew that he was dead.

In Poland there was an order to gather all the children of three years and younger, all together in the center of the village. The men and women of the village, many of them mothers and fathers of the children, were told to dig a big pit. The children were thrown into the pit alive.

The children that were on the top of the pit, after the dirt had been thrown over them, were squirming and still alive. The SS troopers stepped on top of the soil to stop the few remaining feeble movements.

A DISPLACED PERSON *(that I had met while on the street)*: You Americans! You are too easy with the Germans. Do you know what they did to our girls and women? They took all their clothes off, and then cut the hair off their whole body. Not only their head, their whole body! And the women stood there unashamed. Even in their camps, when there weren't any clothes to be had, they were naked. And now, now you Americans go walking with the Germans girls, and given them your chocolate and candy!

CHIAM: The Germans made us urinate in each others' mouths. They fooled us, they beat us, they thought of cruel things to do to us, and to have us do. These two front teeth (*showing me*) were knocked out by a guard. Everyone had a number tattooed on his arm. (*I have seen many of these.*)

ARIYAH: Every time the American planes came over, we were so glad to see them. Yes, we knew that we too might be killed, but we didn't care. What were our lives anyhow? We were being marched along the road one day, when some American planes came over and started to strafe the road. The German guards ran for cover. We, who were very hungry, ran to the carts that had some food in them, and despite the planes that were swooping down on us, started to tear the food out and eat it right there. There were people that were shot, that were standing next to me. People fought each other for a mouthful of food.

At times when the American planes came over, we just stood there and laughed. It made us feel so very good to see the Germans scared and running around. We just didn't care for our lives that much. Just as long as we knew that the Germans would be killed also.

There used to be a siren that would blow every time planes would come over. At first the siren would blow just a few times a day, then almost all day. After a while, it was useless to even blow the siren!

ABRAHAM: When we were transferred from one camp to another, we were crowded so very much into trucks that we could hardly breathe. We were stood upright in the trucks. We were suffocating. You had to be strong to live, as the

273

stronger man just threw out some others, so that he would have room to stand and breathe. If anyone put up any resistance, he was as often as not choked and then thrown out.

HAROLD: I have heard that there were some few Germans that also suffered under the Nazi rule. Did you ever run across them in any of the camps?

CHIAM: Yes, we knew of some of them. Some were political prisoners, others had disobeyed a ruling or some such thing. The Germans were smart, though; the SS would grant the German prisoners a little more food or some slight concession, so that they would do something to the Jews. In that way, they killed two birds with one stone. The German prestige was kept up in that a German was doing something to a Jew, and in the meantime, another Jew or so was being killed or humiliated!

No, there just aren't any good Germans. Don't trust *any* of them. They all have the same bringing up: men, women and children. It is in their heart to be cruel.

HAROLD: (*After talking further, I heard other remarks to the contrary. Despite some of the things that had happened to some of the DPs, they knew the real score of things. That is what surprised me so much.*)

A POLE: I would say that it was in Poland that the Jews suffered the most. Were you to go to Poland now, you could not possibly find a Jewish boy or girl under 18 or 19 years old. It was also in Poland, that they ridiculed the Jew. I saw a Rabbi, all dressed up in his religious outfit, placed on an ox, and made to ride the streets. They (the Germans) took the leather from Jewish religious objects and used it for shoes. The religious cloth that we at one time wore around out necks, we were made to wear on our feet.

ARIYAH: We could go on and on and on, telling you of the many things that happened, and the things that we saw. I know that some people will not believe many of the things we say. Who can blame them? We ourselves, can now hardly believe it. Many times, we just *didn't* want to believe it ourselves.

CONCLUSION

What I have written on these pages, was what was told me by a small group of men that I have met recently. I have heard the same things before from other persons.

Even in Nice, where I went for a vacation, I met a few men that had the number tattooed on their arm. They too had a story to tell like the one I have just told you. They had just been returned from Germany.

Just a couple of days ago, a film was shown to all American soldiers, compulsory, showing some of the atrocities of the Germans. A couple of our temporary KPs (performing the unglamorous Army duty of kitchen patrol), who are DPs, said that the film was just but one percent of what did occur.

Your Harold

THREE PATRIOTS

Exhibit, Norway's Resistance Museum at Akershus, Oslo;
submitted by Ron Petersen

These three Norwegians, after being trained in Great Britain, returned to Norway to organize military resistance. They were arrested in December 1940, condemned to death and executed by Germans outside Akershus in August 1941.

WORLD WAR II:
ILLEGAL NORWEGIAN NEWSPAPERS

Introduction by Pernille Stavseth; documents translated from Norwegian by Astri Grieg Fry

I, Pernille Stavseth, was born five years after World War II, but my father (born in 1903 and old enough to remember two world wars), never let us children forget about the latter war. Nor did my mother, who although still very young during the war (born in 1922), most assuredly was engaged in some surreptitious activities. My parents' combined influence had the long term effect on me of occasionally having nightmares even into adulthood, that I too was the courier of illegal newspapers! This last spring (2015), while going through my father's effects, I discovered a collection of illegal Norwegian newspapers dating from 18 April 1945 through 7 May 1945, offering an insight into just what these bulletins consisted of and the issues they addressed—especially with their emphasis on extreme vigilance as a way of life as well as the stifling of freedom of speech.

Note/Astri Grieg Fry: Once the Allies abandoned Norway's cause only two months into the war, Norway was at the Germans' mercy for the almost five-year duration. Supported by a handful of Norwegian informers, these occupiers—among their multiple other violations—set about confiscating all radios as of late summer of 1941. However, many Norwegians defied the German order, despite deportation and death threats, and concealed their

277

personal radios in order to hear international broadcasts, mostly sent from London's BBC. This intelligence then became published as illegal newspapers in Norway by its Underground Movement, and old and young alike distributed and circulated the pamphlets at great personal risk. Under the strictures of Nazi propaganda and censorship at home, the illegal newspapers formed a vital lifeline to the outside world throughout the war, and the positive effect on Norwegian morale was incalculable.

LONDON 18 April, 1945, 19:30 hours: The Western and Eastern Fronts are now dissolved, reports Max Krull from Berlin! He talks instead of nine new battle zones. Germany is being dismembered quickly. The prisoner total in Ruhr now stands at 309,000 German prisoners. Field marshal Model, the supreme commander in Ruhr, is thought to have committed suicide. He was listed as a war criminal due to among other things his abuses in Letland. In Ruhr the soldiers are throwing down their weapons and rushing in their tanks and vehicles to reach the Allied lines. Northern Holland has been cleaned up except for certain pockets. The Zuiderzee to the northwest has been reached. This afternoon 1000 RAF bombers along with fighters attacked the Helgoland Island in the North Sea German bay in addition to nearby Düne. The British are 50 km. from Hamburg at the mouth of the Elbe River and 25 km. from the lower Elbe. British tanks are approaching Lüneburg. Magdeburg has been seized. In the encircled Leipzig, the Americans now are advancing from the east. They are 50 km. from Dresden and 130 km. from the Russians also to the east. To the North of Magdeburg a slave train was seized with 2400 prisoners, including many Jews. They had been in freight cars for 6 days and nights. There are rumors of great Russian tank concentrations east of Berlin, but Moscow is reporting no details about this from here. Farther south they have crossed the Neisse. Likewise advances to the north, but also from the Stettin area. Suicides among the higher-ranking Germans have begun; there are reports of police chiefs, officers and "judges" who shoot themselves. Over Berlin and Czechoslovakia there is intense bombing. American forces have advanced into Czechoslovakia and are supported by powerful air cover which clears their way. To the south here there are Russians only a few km. away from Brno. Zistersdorf to the northwest of Vienna has been taken. Near Dessau German civilians have joined in the battle. Nürnberg is now almost surrounded and is attacked on three sides. In Italy the 8th Army is rolling across the expanses towards Bologna where the railroad station is now bombarded by long-range artillery. The Poles are positioned here 16 km. from the town, the Americans are closer, but have more difficult terrain in front of them. Argenta has been reached. Churchill announced yesterday in the House of Commons that for various reasons there would be no debate about Poland and the war situation. As war criminals, not only those who have violated the laws of war are considered as such, but also those Nazi leaders who had the responsibility that such actions have happened. In Denmark the Gestapo headquarters in Odense at Fyn was bombed by English mosquitoes. There were approximately 80 Gestapo and Danish collaborators staying there. There were also about 50 prisoners. The number of casualties is unknown. The bombing took place just before the planned evacuation of the Gestapo to another location. The bombers had trained in advance using a simulated model of the site.

[In Norway]the Sørland's (Southern) railroad was shut down for several days due to the blowing up of the Solberg bridge between Kjosen and Drangedal. Toffee Cellulose Factory has been dynamited and considerable wood spirits (a methanol-based alcohol) intended for the Germans destroyed. On 12 April a German ship weighing approx. 500 tons was blown up in the Oslofjord (by saboteurs?). In the Oslo harbor likewise, a ship loaded with food supplies for Germany. Bishop Berggrav had been released by Norwegian Resistance forces, but there is no confirmation as to his whereabouts.

Truman would like to meet with Churchill and Stalin. Eden has held two conferences with Stettinius and will confer with Truman. The new Finnish government consists, according to BBC, mostly of Communists plus Social Democrats. The government indicates a strong leftist movement. There are serious warnings regarding the German informer Otto Dose, aged 31, fluent in Norwegian, operating currently to the north with an unidentified female together with Arne Andresen from Tana. It is re-emphasized that everyone must exercise the greatest caution. Say nothing to anyone, unless it is mandatory. If you are not involved in some work project, then do not try to understand others' occupations, never ask about something you do not need to know, and KEEP YOUR TRAP SHUT! Curiosity and idle chatter have cost enough lives already. It is reported that there are 7 Russian armies which are attacking to the east of Berlin.

BE CAREFUL!

==

LONDON, 30 April 1945, 18:30 hours: From Stockholm it is reported that Count Bernadotte has held a new conference with Himmler yesterday (Sunday) at a castle near Aabenraa near the Danish-German border. Unconfirmed reports claim that he is expected in Stockholm today with new overtures from Himmler. The English press writes today that complete surrender quite simply means total and unconditional surrender without any conditions or demands from the Germans' side. Likewise, that all Nazi leaders and supreme commanders also give themselves up. The fight will go on until all has been taken over and everyone has surrendered and all resistance quelled. They conclude by saying that Himmler probably will try with a new overture. There is no confirmation that Hitler has died of a stroke or is dying (except for the fact that Himmler has suggested the latter). As to the first capitulation proposal's background information, it is reported that while Bernadotte visited Germany regarding certain northbound transports, he was on 21 April requested to join Himmler in Berlin, wherefrom he then was handed his capitulation proposal, which through the Swedish Foreign Office was forwarded to the British and American Legation in Sweden, the matter being conferred with them.

Via Stockholm it is reported as unconfirmed rumors from Oslo that the Quisling government will step down, but that Quisling is attempting to form a new government, a sort of transitional government.

From Denmark it is reported over Moscow that the German soldiers in Norway and Denmark at any moment are awaiting notification to lay down their weapons. Dr. Best in Denmark is said to be negotiating with the Swedes about the surrender.

From Eggedal in Norway there are reports of fighting between the Home Forces and Germans, who in an amount of 100 set out to capture some Norwegians. During the fighting the Germans lost many men, but did take some prisoners and retreated. They returned later with reinforcements, but haven't managed to take more [prisoners].

The destruction in Berlin grows by the hour. Without gas, electricity, water, the civilian population is crowded together in basements like sardines, while the city burns and the houses are shelled and bombed to rubble. The fighting now goes on in the central downtown area: Tiergarten, Wilhemstrasse and Unter den Linden are constantly mentioned in the reports. The German Supreme Commander's communique was released today, but not until 5 o'clock! The Luftwaffe is attempting to furnish reinforcements with parachuters, but these are all—literally —shot down. In Munich there is some lesser fighting during this cleanup. The notorious concentration camp Dachau just to the north of Munich was taken today. 32,000 imprisoned there have been released. 300 SS-executioners have been taken prisoner. In Munich 36,000 Germans have been taken prisoner. Patton's troops have crossed the Isar River in three places over a 100 km.-long stretch between Preisingen and Deggendorf. Ravensburg and Linder in south Bavaria have been taken, the French have crossed Austria's border here and taken Bregens. General Clark reports from Italy that altogether 25 German elite divisions of the best the Germans had are in total disarray and there is now only scattered resistance. Altogether there are 120,000 prisoners here and more pour in. From Venice the 8th Army advances eastward with the Yugoslavians who have taken Trieste, between them all resistance has ceased. The Russians and Allied troops have met each other at two new places by Berlin: by Apollensdorf and by Wittenberg. In Mecklenburg the Russians are advancing and have liberated 27,000 prisoners in Moosburg. There are advances toward Stralsund. East of Hamburg, Montgomery's troops have made a new crossing over the Elbe River by Bleckede, 16 km. southeast of Lauenburg. In the pocket by Bremen the two leading generals there have been taken. The bridge head by Lauenburg is 10 km. deep already. The British are 32 km. from Bremerhafen. By Hamburg, village after village is taken.

283

Holland today received 600 new tons of food supplies by airdrop from England. The House of Commons will debate tomorrow regarding the reports from the German concentration camps. Intelligence from Dachau states that the Americans discovered 50 railway freight cars with corpses from the prisoner camps. South of Weimar the Germans used the prisoners' bodies as road blocks. About Musse [Mussolini] it is said that the execution was necessary for Italy as settlement of the past. Herriot who was released last week has arrived in Moscow. The *Times* writes that, from the military point of view, Germany has reached the capitulation phase long ago; the fighting continuation is due to the maniacal fanaticism and blindness.

[Norway's] Home Front's Leadership (HL) has sent out directive No. 1 under the new, existing situation which specifies: 1) Avoid congregating. Do not participate in demonstrations of any kind. Do not behave provocatively. 2) Distribute correct reports from the London radio, observe and commit to paper, do not trust your memory. 3) Do not relax the usual precautions. Gestapo will work to the very end.

REMEMBER: CALMNESS—DIGNITY—DISCIPLINE

Exercise caution!

==

REMEMBER: CALMNESS DIGNITY DISCIPLINE

LONDON, 3 May 1945, 12:00 hours: British troops advance at 13:00 hours into Hamburg, which by the Germans has been declared an open city. Berlin has been destroyed worse than Stalingrad. An epidemic of suicides. Following the report of Hitler's suicide, his ghost is also dead. General Dempsey's troops have met the Russians, east of Wismar by the Baltic Sea.

12:15 hours: The Allied Supreme Command has declared a curfew for all Germans in Hamburg, with the exception of gas, electrical and water supply workers. Confusion in Denmark. Extensive air attacks on Kiel last night. From Admiral Dönitz via Hamburg, a communique has been sent that Prague has been declared a field hospital city. The new German Army Chief of Staff, Generalstabschef Krebs, committed suicide along with Göbbels. What has become of Keitel? This Tuesday the free newspapers in Denmark were printed, ready for distribution, but the delivery was stopped.

15:00 hours: The Allies have taken Rangoon. Unconfirmed Stockholm's rumors say that Terboven and Best are meeting with Dönitz in Denmark.

17:00 hours: Allied planes energetically bomb German transports moving northward to Denmark. Smaller boats are leaving the Schleswig-Holstein harbors, northbound. Considerable shooting in Copenhagen last night. The Prague radio has made no announcement regarding Dönitz' report that Prague should be a "hospital city"(?). The Supreme Commander in Czechoslovakia is von Schörner. He has 2 1/2 million men. The German minister in

Stockholm states that he has no official confirmation regarding Hitler's death and Dönitz' assumption of power. With Hitler's death he considers that he has been released from his oath of allegiance. He has no connection with Germany. Oldenburg is taken. Passau on the Austrian border is taken.

<u>18:00 hours</u>: 10 km. from Innsbruck—The *gauleiter,* a regional Nazi party leader, has declared it an open city and has given orders that no bridges are to be blown up. Yesterday 18 German generals and 3 field marshals were taken prisoner. Trieste is now cleaned up. Before the surrender in Italy, 230,000 prisoners were taken in this offensive. Churchill was not at his place in the House of Commons today. In his place Sir John Anderson answered the questions that were put to the government.

<u>18:15 hours</u>: The rumor that Best is conferring with Dönitz remains. The tendencies of surrender in Denmark are due to confusion among the German commanders following the development of the last few days. In addition to the surrender of the Italian army, today there is the message that general Freiberg in Trieste has surrendered with the garrison there. Of the final battle in Italy, the English press declares: "The best equipped of the German armies have been completely defeated by the swift offensive that General Clark executed under Field Marshal Alexander's leadership." The affair is considered to be the greatest military surrender in the history of the world. Denmark's Freedom Council disapproves of the Danish authorities who, after the local commanders' surrender in certain

places, established normal conditions; and emphasizes that no one must act independently, but wait until executives issue their orders.

<u>18:30 hours</u>: A precaution to the Home Front from its leaders, No. 2, emphasizes that Norwegians must be vigilant regarding provocations, it is Germans who want to hinder any organized capitulation in Norway and who are interested in creating disturbances. Do not roam around in the streets. Continue your daily work, it is important that everything continues normally. Disregard all rumors and heed what is reported from London and our authentic authorities. Exemplify CALMNESS DIGNITY DISCIPLINE, etc. It appears that the Germans are trying to hold the reins tightly in Norway and Denmark right up until the final outcome. The Russians and Americans have met each other 6 km. south-east of Ludwigslust, plus three other places farther south. The advance toward the Baltic Sea was undertaken at a tremendous tempo, which caused complete confusion among the German troops. Two entire divisions surrendered here. The British took 100,000 prisoners in this area. The Russians took 100,000 prisoners during Berlin's surrender yesterday.

Along the Inn River on the Austrian border, the Americans hold 120 km. They are somewhere 40 km. east of the river. After the surrender of the Italian army, besides Italy, the areas of Salzburg, Vorarlberg, and parts of Kärnten and Steiermark, the Germans have only troops in the Donau valley left in Austria. They are positioned between the

Russians and Americans who approach each other from both sides.

BE CAREFUL

==

LONDON, 6 May 1945, 18:00 hours: A report in German: The liberation of Norway is expected to be imminent. Allied tanks approach Prague from the west and the Russians are already positioned 200 km. east of the city. At Narvik Allied naval forces and planes have attacked a submarine supply ship and several other Germans warships which have been sunk or damaged. Two planes are missing, the Allied warships have returned undamaged. Dr. Frick, the former Reich Protector of Bohemia and Moravia, has been taken prisoner.

18:14 hours: The liberation of Norway is now imminent. Negotiations about the transfer of power in Bohemia and Moravia to the Czechoslovakian government is underway. At 6 o'clock this morning orders were issued for a ceasefire in Prague. Tito reports of advances along the entire Croation Front. In Schleswig-Holstein there are now over 2,000,000 German refugees. The Germans have reported that they don't have food for themselves for even ten days, but Montgomery has declared that, whatever food can be obtained, first and foremost will be issued to the population of Holland, Denmark—should anyone lack food it will be the Germans first, he said. Daladier, Reynaud and others were released from a secret camp in a remote Alpine location. Leon Blum was removed from there only a few hours before the Americans came. In Milan the military tribunal has executed about 1000 fascists. The Japanese prime minister has accused Germany today of having betrayed the Tripartite Pact by capitulating and threatened to annul all its pacts with Germany if it sues for peace with USA and England.

The Justice Department in London reports that it is of the greatest importance that the official financial records and other official documents are preserved. There is reason to fear that some of the country's traitors wish to see these proofs of their deeds removed. Having the address of such persons, one will certainly prevent that records or archive documents are altered or destroyed. By official decree, strict punishments from 2 till 8 years and up to 12 years are in force if considerable damage has been done. This includes documents concerning the State as well as the municipalities.

It is reported that a great number of planes landed at an airport near Oslo yesterday and last night, they came partly from Denmark and partly from northern Germany.

It has been denied that Dönitz is in Oslo, he is somewhere else altogether. Øksnevad spoke from Stockholm over BBC, saying that the Swedes are expecting a considerable number of German guests traveling en route. It is impossible to say anything definite about all the rumors that are spread. The Swedish newspapers now only have Norway to inflict their oversized headlines on. From some Fronts there are no reports. There is only one capital in

Europe which has not been liberated, namely Oslo. There are warnings against all rumors, disregarding the size of the headlines or the extent of the rumors. The greatest caution must be exercised. Jonas Lie still suffers from lust and bloodthirstiness, he still has Germans backing him up, plus Rogstad. Quisling has hardly anything to say in his own defense, but he prefers capitulation rather than be Terboven's slave. If there is no organized capitulation in Norway, the Allies will intervene quickly. Both Norwegians and the German Wehrmacht soldiers are expected to remain calm, but hardly the Nazis and the SS. One must be aware that with a capitulation, the dangers are not over, but clear directives will be issued.

19:00 hours: The count of German prisoners in the West has reached a total of 5,000,000. The Czechoslovakian government has been flown back home. An English parliamentary commentator characterized the situation among the parliament members this week thus: "You know how it is, when you go waiting for something to happen, then you just languish by the tea-urn and wait for news." So it is for all of us.

20:00 hours: Churchill will give a speech on 10 May in observation of the five-year anniversary of his appointment as prime minister. —The Norwegian government has its plans for the cessation of the occupation formulated. An Allied military commission will immediately come here and take over. Included in this will be Norwegian members and the leadership of the commission will be placed in the hands of Crown Prince Olav. The government then will probably step down and a new government comprised of all the political parties will be appointed. The foreign minister's position will probably be relegated to someone who can preserve the continuity with the other powers. (This was reported in the Danish communique.)

REMEMBER: BE CAREFUL

==

EXEMPLIFY: DIGNITY —CALMNESS — DISCIPLINE LONDON, 7 May 1945, 12:15 hours (Danish broadcast): The war is quickly approaching its conclusion. And it is said that one at any hour can expect Germany's final unconditional capitulation to Great Britain, USA and Russia. A communique regarding Norway's liberation can also be expected soonest. (The radio announcer interrupted here with the following report for Norwegian listeners:) We have been requested to inform the Norwegian listeners that there at the moment is nothing new regarding Norway. The British government is holding ongoing meetings. The three great powers are in constant contact to discuss the latest details. Every moment a decision is expected, writes the Times today. Rumors from Stockholm suggest that the German minister in Sweden, Dr. Hans Thomsen has been in a meeting at the Norwegian border with the German Armed Forces Commander of Norway, General Böhme. And newspapers in Stockholm provided unconfirmed rumors that great German troop forces are positioned along the Swedish border to be interned there once the capitulation

291

takes effect. In Denmark it has been decided to impose the death penalty for the country's traitors. Terboven has resigned and Rediess has been deposed, allegedly. The German military in Norway is in power at the moment. Molotov is thought to have returned to Moscow. King Leopold will abdicate. 6,968,000 men will participate in the last attack on Japan.

12:30 hours (Norwegian report from New York over BBC): We continue to stress that there is no official report regarding Norway.

CONTINUE TO REMAIN CAUTIOUS

Oslo news: The Germans today conducted raids in a couple of houses by Olav Kyrre's Square.

BE CAREFUL

===

FINAL WAR EDITION

LONDON, 7 MAY 1945, 15:00 hours: It is reported that the German Foreign Minister Krosigk, by the sending of the capitulation message to the German people over Flensburg radio today, said that it was Grand Admiral Dönitz who had given the German supreme command orders to unconditionally capitulate with all German forces. Krosigk said that he spoke as the leading minister in the German government which by Dönitz had as assignment to address these matters of war. 50 minutes after this report from Krosigk was sent out, Oslo Kringkasting began to broadcast the same message. Prague radio continued meanwhile to report that the battle there would continue until the German troops were rescued by the Germans. In London crowds are beginning to assemble in Downing Street, said a [radio] spokesperson "to hear the order of ceasing fire." At the end of the message he added: "The moment for Mr. Churchill's speech is now very near."

(The above-mentioned report from Prague was sent from the one and only radio station the Germans still have.)

18:00 hours (Broadcast in German from BBC, London): The complete German capitulation was signed in Eisenhower's headquarters at 2:41 hours this last night. On behalf of the Wehrmacht, Colonel General Jodl signed (he was formerly Hitler's inside man within the Supreme Command).

Eisenhower was not present, but received the German negotiators Colonel General Jodl and General Admiral Friedeberg immediately afterwards. Eisenhower asked them in sharp and no uncertain terms if they understood the conditions and if these would be adhered to. The Germans replied that, yes, they understood them and that they would be fulfilled. Jodl stated moreover: "By this signing are the German armed forces delivered up to the mercy of the victors." Between London, Washington and Moscow there have today been numerous telephone conversations and Churchill confers with his Cabinet. Any official confirmation is still pending. It will consist of a governmental act so that the declaration must stem from the three heads of state, in the three leading Allied powers. The battles in Prague have not ceased, but the Czech government has over BBC sent out a message to the German forces in Czechoslovakia that, if they continue the fight, they will according to national law be treated as terrorists.

(From where we are listening, we see now the area's youngsters run joyfully about on the street and wave their Norwegian flags in the lovely May sunshine under a high blue sky with a light green veil over the trees. The report that the war actually is over, has spread and taken root in everyone, and we await now just that they will raise the flag in the region as well.)

19:00 hours: A number of German generals who were taken prisoner in Berlin declare that Hitler committed suicide and in the Reich Chancellery's ruins one digs for the corpse. From one of the remaining German pockets by the Elbe River it is reported that the Germans now are constructing a crossing over the river so as to soonest be taken prisoner by the Americans. The capitulation was signed tonight in Rheims in France, where Eisenhower has his headquarters in a small school building.

20:00 hours (Danish broadcast from BBC): It is announced that Mr. Churchill will speak over the radio on Tuesday at 15:00 hours and King George at 21:00 hours. In England it is a holiday tomorrow and Wednesday.

Commentary: The final end of the war must therefore be considered confirmed.—V-Day is therefore Tuesday, 8 May 1945.

Made in the USA
San Bernardino, CA
22 October 2015